T0299226

Systems Thinking and Sustainable Healthcare Delivery

The Sustainable Development Goal 3 seeks to ensure health and well-being for all at every stage of life. This book discusses how to strengthen our healthcare systems and ensure sustainable community healthcare delivery by using systems thinking, an approach to understanding complex interactions of individual system elements in nature.

Financing and manpower planning are integral processes to achieve health for all in the world. Adopting the Framework for Action of the World Health Organization for Strengthening Health Systems to Improve Health Outcomes, this book reviews and discusses, illustrated by case examples, the building blocks of healthcare systems, namely financing, human resources, management strategies and leadership and governance in the context of accessibility, coverage, quality and safety of community health services to achieve selected targets in SDG 3 in the context of global health.

This book will be of interest to those who are researching sustainable healthcare systems, as well as policymakers and healthcare professionals.

Ben Y. F. Fong is a Specialist in Community Medicine, holding honorary Clinical Associate Professorship at the two local medical schools in Hong Kong, China. He is currently the Professor of Practice (Health Studies) and Associate Division Head of the Division of Science, Engineering, and Health Studies, and Director of the Centre for Ageing and Healthcare Management Research of the College of Professional and Continuing Education at The Hong Kong Polytechnic University. He has contributed to publications, including *Primary Care Revisited: Interdisciplinary Perspectives for a New Era* (as lead editor, published in 2020), a training manual for general practitioners in China published by the People's Medical Publishing House in Beijing (as co-editor, published in 2020), over 30 health books in Chinese and 40 journal papers.

Routledge Focus on Business and Management

The fields of business and management have grown exponentially as areas of research and education. This growth presents challenges for readers trying to keep up with the latest important insights. *Routledge Focus on Business and Management* presents small books on big topics and how they intersect with the world of business research.

Individually, each title in the series provides coverage of a key academic topic, whilst collectively, the series forms a comprehensive collection across the business disciplines.

Neuroscience and Entrepreneurship Research
Researching Brain-Driven Entrepreneurship
Víctor Pérez Centeno

Proposal Writing for Business Research Projects
Peter Samuels

Systems Thinking and Sustainable Healthcare Delivery
Ben Y. F. Fong

Gender Diversity and Inclusion at Work
Divergent Views from Turkey
Zeynep Özsoy, Mustafa Senyücel and Beyza Oba

Management and Visualisation
Seeing Beyond the Strategic
Gordon Fletcher

For more information about this series, please visit: www.routledge.com/Routledge-Focus-on-Business-and-Management/book-series/FBM

Systems Thinking and Sustainable Healthcare Delivery

Ben Y. F. Fong

WITH CONTRIBUTIONS FROM
FOWIE NG, KAR-WAI TONG, WANG-KIN CHIU,
TOMMY K. C. NG, AND HILARY H. L. YEE

Routledge
Taylor & Francis Group

LONDON AND NEW YORK

First published 2023
by Routledge
4 Park Square, Milton Park, Abingdon, Oxon OX14 4RN

and by Routledge
605 Third Avenue, New York, NY 10158

Routledge is an imprint of the Taylor & Francis Group, an informa business

British Library Cataloguing-in-Publication Data
A catalogue record for this book is available from the British Library

ISBN: 9781032305363 (hbk)
ISBN: 9781032305370 (pbk)
ISBN: 9781003305637 (ebk)

DOI: 10.4324/9781003305637

Typeset in Times New Roman
by codeMantra

Contents

Figures

Author and Co-Authors

Author

Ben Y. F. Fong is a Specialist in Community Medicine, graduated in Medicine from the University of Sydney, Australia, where he also obtained his Master's degree in public health. He has held senior management positions at Prince Henry Hospital, a teaching hospital of the University of New South Wales, Australia, as well as Ruttonjee Hospital and Union Hospital in Hong Kong, China. He is currently the Professor of Practice (Health Studies) and Associate Division Head of the Division of Science, Engineering and Health Studies, and Director of the Centre for Ageing and Healthcare Management Research (CAHMR) of the College of Professional and Continuing Education, The Hong Kong Polytechnic University. He is Honorary Clinical Associate Professor in Family Medicine at both The Chinese University of Hong Kong (CUHK) and The University of Hong Kong, and at the School of Chinese Medicine of CUHK, as well as Adjunct Professor in Public Health & Tropical Medicine in the College of Public Health, Medical and Veterinary Sciences at James Cook University, Australia. He has contributed to publications as lead editor of three books, including recent titles of "Routledge Handbook of Public Health and the Community" in 2021 and "Primary Care Revisited – Interdisciplinary Perspectives for a New Era" in 2020, over 30 health books in Chinese and 40 journal papers.

https://directory.cpce-polyu.edu.hk/staff-directory/en/cpce/cpce-acadiv-sehs-acastf/ben-fong

Co-authors

Wang-Kin Chiu received his Bachelor of Science (first class honours) degree and a PhD in chemistry from the Chinese University of Hong Kong. He is a Senior Lecturer at the College of Professional and Continuing Education (CPCE) of the Hong Kong Polytechnic University (PolyU). He is currently serving as the Assistant Program Leader of the Associate in Health Studies and the Assistant Award Leader of the Bachelor of Science (honours) in Applied Sciences (health studies). He is a Management Committee Member of the Centre for Ageing and Healthcare Management Research at PolyU CPCE and a Member of the CPCE Centre for Pedagogic Research at PolyU CPCE. He is a Fellow of the Hong Kong College of Community Health Practitioners and a Member of the American Chemical Society.

Fowie Ng is currently Associate Professor at the School of Management of Tung Wah College. He received his PhD in Health Policy and Management from the University of Hull in the UK. He has extensive teaching, research and management experiences at Hong Kong Polytechnic University, School of Professional Education and Executive Development at The Hong Kong Polytechnic University, University of Hong Kong (HKUSPACE), The Chinese University of Hong Kong (CUSCS), Hong Kong Baptist University SCE, CityU SCOPE, Open University of Hong Kong and the University of Sunderland. Dr. Ng is Fellow of the Australasian College of Health Service Management, Hong Kong College of Health Service Executives and the Hong Kong College of Community Health Practitioners.

Tommy K. C. Ng is the Project Associate in the Centre for Ageing and Healthcare Management Research (CAHMR) of CPCE at The Hong Kong Polytechnic University. In this position at CAHMR, he is actively involved in research related to health topics and is responsible for organising different research activities, including conferences, research seminars and methodology workshops. He has recently published research papers in international journals. His research interests include primary care and public health.

Kar-wai Tong has had multi-disciplinary exposure. He served the healthcare and social care sectors as a management staff for over a decade. He received legal training in Hong Kong and the UK. In particular, he holds a degree of Doctor of Juridical Science (Hong Kong) with a focus on medico-legal liabilities of practising tele-health. Kar-wai was called to the Bar (England and Wales). He is also an enrolled barrister and solicitor (New Zealand) (non-practicing), a legal practitioner (New South Wales, Australia) (non-practicing), a member of the Chartered Institute of Arbitrators (UK), and an accredited general mediator (Hong Kong). He was awarded a scholarship for another comparative PhD study in the UK with a theme of Confucian happiness and he is a graduand as of this writing. Kar-wai has also been teaching at universities on a part-time basis. His research interests include telehealth, medico-legal liabilities, healthcare and social policies, human rights, legal issues in education and happiness.

Hilary H. L. Yee received her Bachelor of Science (Psychology) from Swansea University in the United Kingdom. She is the Research Associate in the Department of Rehabilitation Science at The Hong Kong Polytechnic University. She has participated in several journal papers on various topics, including palliative care, elderly home safety, lifelong education and service learning to older adults, as well as book chapters in primary care and public health. Her research interests include rehabilitation services and primary healthcare.

1 Systems Thinking for Sustainable Healthcare Systems

Wang-Kin Chiu and Ben Y. F. Fong

Introduction

Systems thinking has emerged as a platform for understanding the complexity of a system, including the dynamic interactions of components within the system and the complicated relationships with other systems. The systems approach is of particular value when the linear approach of cause-and-effect thinking leads to inefficiency or even failure of providing comprehensive solutions, arising from different characteristics of complex systems such as ambiguity, emergence, interconnectivity, policy interventions and other socio-economic factors (Hossain et al., 2020). In the past decades, there have been extensive studies reporting the applications of systems thinking in various domains. For example, a recent review study by Wang et al. (2022) has investigated and analysed social commerce systems through a systems thinking perspective, which contributed to the development of a conceptual framework to better understand the interconnections between different components in the social commerce process. In the engineering discipline, through visualising the interconnectedness between constituent components as well as identifying the variations and potential impacts over time, systems thinking research aims at recognising both the technical and contextual factors in engineering work for making appropriate designs and providing effective solutions (Dugan et al., 2021).

During recent years, various studies have examined the adoption of systems science in the healthcare discipline, with surging interest in the applicability of systems-based approaches to public health (Bagnall et al., 2019; Carey et al., 2015). Due to the intrinsic complexity of public health problems, systems thinking has been recognised to have critical roles in addressing major challenges in public health. In addition, the operations of healthcare systems being complicated

DOI: 10.4324/9781003305637-1

by the interconnections with many other systems have further led to suggestions put forward for the prominent need of a complex systems model, adopting a variety of approaches to design, implement and evaluate relevant policy measures and interventions, for improvement of public health (Rutter et al., 2017). After all, public health problems such as obesity are complex and multicausal, which cannot necessarily and simply be solved with one single intervention. To achieve more meaningful impacts through interventions, interacting factors within a system need to be reshaped for generation of a more desirable set of outcomes. A systems thinking approach is therefore important in the health sector, especially in the case of weaker health systems for which more complex interventions are expected to lead to profound effects across the system (De Savigny & Adam, 2009).

To apply such an approach in the health system, ten steps have been proposed as a real-world guidance in the report published by the World Health Organization (WHO), which is entitled Systems Thinking for Health Systems Strengthening (De Savigny & Adam, 2009). The ten steps were grouped into two categories, namely intervention design and evaluation design. The first four steps enclosed in intervention design are: (1) convene stakeholders, (2) collectively brainstorm, (3) conceptualise effects and (4) adapt and redesign; while the six steps in the evaluation design category are: (5) determine indicators, (6) choose methods, (7) select design,; (8) develop plan, (9) set budget and (10) source funding. While the steps are indicative and the benefits of systems thinking are widely advocated, it is noteworthy that the application of systems thinking does not mean that overcoming weakness and resolving problems will come naturally or easily. Therefore, experience from the applications of systems thinking in different situations will be an asset to both academicians, policymakers and practitioners. In this chapter, case studies and reports from different countries such as China and Canada, which are related to the applications of systems thinking approach in major health issues and related strategies, will be reviewed. Furthermore, knowledge in systems thinking with respect to the building blocks of the WHO health system framework and their application in achieving sustainable healthcare systems will be discussed with reference to Sustainable Development Goal (SDG) 3.

Tools for Applying Systems Thinking

There have been extensive applications of systems thinking in different domains reported in the past decades. One of the commonly adopted systems thinking tools is the casual loop diagram (CLD). A casual diagram is one which is graphically depicted and created based on the interacting factors and elements of a system, as well as the interconnections between these components (Lagarda-Leyva & Ruiz, 2019). The development of a casual model is a critical process in system dynamics methodology which considers the exogenous and endogenous variables while incorporating parameters having direct impact on the behaviour of one or more interacting variables within a system. Compared with a linguistic description, a casual diagram offers the advantage of a higher degree of formality but has a lower precision than a mathematical equation. Comparatively, a casual diagram also encompasses the concept of feedback visualised as circular chains of influence, facilitating the understanding and explanations of specific behaviours of a model structure (Guo et al., 2019).

Overall, graphical representations are frequently observed in studies related to systems thinking application. In addition to CLDs, another visualisation tool is the system-oriented concept map extension (SOCME) diagrams, which serve as graphical tools for conceptualising systems thinking in education domain. Recent studies have also reported the design of these diagrams as educational resources connecting the chemical, human health and environmental systems, where inter-disciplinary collaborative efforts of integrating sustainability in education have been further advocated (Chiu et al., 2022; Mahaffy et al., 2019a; Wissinger et al., 2021).

Applying Systems Thinking in Health Domains

Systems Thinking to Support Sustainable Health Systems

Recently, Lagarda-Leyva & Ruiz (2019) have reported the use of a systems thinking model focusing on the long-term bearability of the system aiming to support a sustainable healthcare system in the Province of Québec, Canada. The study describes the work involved in the first phase of systems dynamics methodology, which is the conceptualisation phase utilising casual diagrams for the analysis of the relationships and influences among selected entities. The four entities, which self-regulate and interact to give the care-providing system, were identified and their interrelationships were studied. The four entities are: (1) universities, (2) hospitals and doctors, (3) the ministry and (4) the society. The analysis stage in relation to the four entities consisted of three distinct phases, the objectives of which were: (1) to determine the critical parameters and variables for each identified entity, (2) to develop a specific CLD for each entity and (3) to integrate the individual casual diagrams from the second phase for compilation of the overall system diagram. In the first place, regarding the determination of the critical parameters and variables for each specific entity, relevant factors were considered and selected based on theoretical research of empirical studies and stakeholder experience. For example, regarding the parameters for the entity of Québec society, the parameter list included birth rate, average life expectancy, percentage of people at work and immigration rate, respectively. As for the entity of hospitals, the listed parameters were concentration rate of medical doctors in rural areas, concentration rate of medical doctors in urban areas, contract rate per time according to the types of medical doctors, number of hospitals in Québec and the number of doctors per hospital.

After the first phase, the second phase involved the development of each entity based on the parameters and variables. To better understand the interactions and influences among the variables, the parameters were used to generate the dynamics for each variable involved, and the specific casual diagrams for each of the four entities were constructed. These casual diagrams were then integrated in the final phase to give the CLD for the whole system which showed all four entities. This was important to provide all stakeholders with a comprehensive global view, enabling them to observe their roles and the interactions with different systems, which was essential to make adjustments to the constructed model before advancing to the simulation stage. It is noteworthy that with appropriate adjustments, the model is of potential for replication in other countries having the four entities analysed in the case of Québec, Canada.

In addition, there are other examples advancing the applications of systems thinking in health. It has significant implications, especially for countries having a growing number of rapid and interconnected changes for development of health system, to understand and analyse the system performance from a wider perspective and in its broader context (Leischow & Milstein, 2006; Zhang et al., 2014). Meanwhile, there have been increasing studies in applying concepts of complex adaptive systems for health system analysis, which incorporate the understanding of healthcare systems as complex adaptive systems, with components interacting in apparently random manners (Holland, 2006; Pype et al., 2018). Examples include various case studies which applied the concepts of complex adaptive systems to different areas of health system performance, including palliative care (Munday et al., 2003), primary care (Litaker et al., 2006), health care and services delivery systems (Tan et al., 2005), understanding of global health governance (Hill, 2011) and in other health system areas (Best et al., 2012).

The concepts of complex adaptive systems were also applied to study how institutional arrangements would affect policy translation into changes in system behaviour. For example, Xiao et al. (2013) have applied the concepts to explore the implementation of policy in China regarding essential drugs. Their study also suggests that the emergence of adaptive and self-organised behaviour are important factors to be considered in the management of policy changes in rural China, with a systems thinking approach to address many non-linear changes. Furthermore, regarding sustainable health system development, the concepts of complex adaptive systems, in conjunction with the lens of resilience thinking which offer a solid framework to examine the dynamic, complex and long process of system changes, are essential to studies of changes in social-ecological systems (Folke et al., 2010). From the perspective of system evolution, it is essential to analyse and understand the impact of individual adaptations for achievement of system goals, system resilience as well as choices of system transition (Van der Brugge & Van Raak, 2007). These concepts were applied in the review study by Zhang et al. (2014), which investigated the evolution of Cooperative Medical System and New Cooperative Medical System as a case study of the long and complex process of rural China health system development. The retrospective study gives a comprehensive review on the development of the rural health system over a duration of three and half decades, which provides important insights regarding the challenges in management over the adaptation of a sustainable health system faced with a rapidly evolving context. Overall, more research studies on the applications of complex adaptive systems, as well as on the management of health system transition and adaptation to changing contexts are required.

SDG 3 and Systems Thinking

Applications of systems thinking are also significantly related to achievement of SDGs, which were set up in 2015 by the United Nations. In particular, considering the complexity of public health and the need of multisectoral approaches, systems thinking is important for achieving SDG 3. Although the main focus of SDG 3 is explicitly on good health and well-being which aims to ensure healthy lives and promote well-being for all at all ages, SDG 3 is connected with almost all other goals (Hussain et al., 2020; Reynolds et al., 2018). Identifying a wide range of health policy and systems research priorities is crucial for policymakers to develop and strengthen primary health care and community-based health systems. Notably, it has been further emphasised to engage participants from outside the health sector in both research investigations and policymaking processes to achieve health-related goals (Brolan et al., 2019).

A systems thinking approach is also important for facilitating intersectoral efforts in achieving sustainable health systems while it is necessary to have more investigations for practical interventions and measures leading to significant engagement of sectors and implementation of effective policies specific to the SDGs. In recent years, there have been extensive studies regarding the applications of systems thinking in relation to public health (Chughtai & Blanchet, 2017). In fact, the use of systems thinking has also been extended to urban health research and sustainable healthy cities (Cristiano & Zilio, 2021). For example, Peters (2014) has discussed the added values of applying systems thinking in the contexts of public health research and design of interventions to improve public health. Adopting a participatory approach based on the Sustainability Framework, Sarriot et al. (2014) have applied systems thinking to generate creative thinking from various stakeholders for health system improvement in Northern Bangladesh. Furthermore, casual diagrams have been used in various studies. In 2014, Rwashana et al. (2014) reported the use of CLDs to understand the dynamics of neonatal mortality in Uganda. Using the same approach, Agyepong et al. (2014) have assessed the Ghana National Health Insurance Scheme focusing on the influence of provider payment methods on incentives and behaviour.

It is noteworthy that in addition to direct applications of systems thinking in health research and policy implementation, systems thinking is of promising prospects in education for sustainable development. The current situations, including the ageing population and increasing prevalence of chronic diseases, have been posing significant challenges for sustaining the already heavily loaded healthcare systems around the world (Braithwaite et al., 2019; Fong et al., 2021). Circumstances like increasing levels of pollution which lead to ongoing deterioration of the environment are threatening human health and well-being, particularly for the older adults which are more vulnerable to the associated health impacts, further increasing the burden to healthcare systems (Chiu & Fong, 2022; Simoni et al., 2015). As also indicated in Target 3.9 of SDG 3 aiming for a substantial reduction of deaths and illnesses from hazardous chemicals and pollution of the environment, to ensure the long-term development of sustainable healthcare systems, these health risk factors, posing significant challenges to sustain healthcare systems, should not be overlooked (Chiu et al., 2022). Education for a green and sustainable environment is also fundamental to sustain health systems and has attracted growing interests in the recent years. For example, the practice of chemistry and development of chemical technology have profound impacts on various interconnected systems, with the material basis of a sustainable environment being highly dependent on different chemical processes and products (Zimmerman et al., 2020). Meanwhile, it has been recognised that education for a sustainable environment is important in cultivating the young generations to design and develop green processes and technologies, for which a systems thinking mindset would also have significant contributions to decision-making and development of a comprehensive understanding for inter-disciplinary collaborations in the invention of a sustainable future (Chiu et al., 2022; Zuin et al., 2021).

Recently, there have been calls for immediate actions for adopting the SDGs as a central concern in re-orientation of chemistry education and development of relevant resources (Mahaffy et al., 2019b; Matlin et al., 2015). Although studies related to the development of relevant educational resources are only of limited amount, the promising educational prospects of implementing inter-disciplinary approaches as informed by systems thinking have been extensively discussed while there have also been growing reports of incorporating systems thinking supported with emerging technologies in the pedagogic design of chemistry education (Chiu, 2021; Hurst, 2020). While it is acknowledged that the reductionist approach adopted in the teaching of science subjects has significant contributions to advancing scientific knowledge and discoveries, a systems thinking approach to achieve the visualisation of interconnections between chemical systems and other systems is much needed in the context of education for addressing the global challenges such as climate change and contaminations of the environment, which have serious implications over the sustainability of healthcare systems (Holme, 2020; Orgill et al., 2019). Recent studies have also focused on inter-disciplinary collaborations to investigate the adoption of systems thinking in education (Constable et al., 2019; Schultz et al., 2021). In 2019, Fowler et al. have reported a study which adopted systems thinking in the pedagogic design of STEM educational strategies incorporated with perspectives among academicians, policymakers, and the general public. Recently, an inter-disciplinary collaboration between disciplines of health and chemical science was reported which involved the design of a SOCME diagram for a greenhouse gas, methane (Chiu et al., 2022). Another example focusing on the use of SOCME diagrams to illustrate the interconnections of the Haber process, a well-known industrial process with wide applications to the society, was reported (Mahaffy et al., 2019a). To sum up, these studies have presented the efforts for incorporation of systems thinking in education. They also provide valuable resources to facilitate education for sustainable environment.

In addition to education of fundamental science subjects, efforts in other domains of education are also important for achieving sustainable healthcare systems. These include educational research and policy studies with the goal of addressing the increasing challenges to health systems. For example, resource management education is important for the heavily loaded health systems. Adopting a systems thinking framework incorporated with the concepts of circular economy, it is expected that the inter-disciplinary work across different disciplines of business, health and science education would contribute to reduction of waste and emission generation, as well as resource usage, which are crucial to sustainable healthcare systems and also a green environment (Kümmerer et al., 2020; Zuin et al., 2021). Regarding policymaking education, Minyard et al. (2014) have applied systems thinking in an educational initiative aiming to improve policymaking processes by the provision of training programmes to legislators. The feature of the educational programme involved the use of systems thinking for a comprehensive and broad analysis of the influences of policy on health systems and public health. The findings support that educational programmes incorporated with systems thinking are having promising potential in policymaker education, and they are also important in facilitating the understanding of disparate health status due to diversified populations. Overall, the systems thinking framework is having increasing roles in the design of health-related courses while more investigations are necessary for further development of educational resources to be adopted in education incorporated with systems thinking approaches.

Health System Resilience and COVID-19

Health system resilience is an important factor affecting the sustainability of sustainable healthcare systems. Originated from the ecological sciences, the concept of resilience is defined in terms of the amount of change a system can adapt to while the same controls on structures and functions are maintained (Blanchet & James, 2013). With increasing popularity in global public health, health system resilience is recognised as a critical concept for global health in a recent editorial published in the Bulletin of WHO (Kutzin & Sparkes, 2016).

In the field of disaster management, conceptualisation of resilience has attracted increasing attentions over the recent years (Mavhura, 2017). Disaster resilience has been viewed as the capacity of a community or a social system to prepare for, respond to and recover quickly from the impacts of a disaster. The concepts of disaster resilience are not just referring to how fast a society recovers from the disaster impacts. In addition, the ability of the community to learn to cope with and adapt to hazards, as well as the underlying management capacity of the system and its actors to respond to changes, are also emphasised (Blanchet et al., 2017; Mayunga, 2007). Recently, optimisation models for effective restructuring and reformatting of hospital and healthcare facilities under emergency situations have been suggested which aim at reducing the number of casualties in disaster events (Aghapour et al., 2019). The results of a recent review have also supported the importance of the assessment of hospital disaster resilience for management to identify the areas of vulnerability within a hospital's infrastructure as well as to inform improvement strategies for calamitous situations (Luke et al., 2021).

During the recent decades, disaster operations management and healthcare management have become increasingly important due to more frequent occurrence of disasters such as earthquakes, cyclones, floods and pandemic of infectious diseases (Aghapour et al., 2019; Mavhura, 2017). Many rural communities are facing serious threats of climate-related disasters arising from extreme weather events due to climate change and high levels of poverty. The devastating impacts of disasters on human life, hospital facilities and healthcare services delivery, infrastructure and resources are also significantly destroying the sustainability of healthcare systems. Under all these circumstances, it has been widely recognised as a top agenda for the global community to help develop more resilient health systems (Blanchet et al., 2017). Strengthening the capability of health systems for the management and governance of resilience is crucial to the effective delivery of preventative and curative healthcare services to the public.

In a recent study based on health systems thinking and complexity science, Blanchet et al. (2017) have presented a new conceptual framework on resilience governance incorporated with the three defined levels of resilience, namely, the absorptive capacity, adaptive capacity and transformative capacity. In the new framework, four dimensions to manage health system resilience have been proposed focusing on the mechanisms of how health system actors collect and interpret complex information, the strategies used by health system actors to manage uncertainty, the interconnections of health systems with other systems, as well as the approaches of health systems to develop institutions and norms which are socially and contextually acceptable. The framework is of promising use by health systems researchers, health practitioners and policymakers for exploring the characteristics of resilient health systems and formulating context-specific, evidence-based and comprehensive approaches for health resilience enhancement.

Furthermore, systems thinking also finds its wide applications in policy recommendations about disaster management. These studies are of special values to populations in the Asia-Pacific regions considering the vulnerability of Asian continent to natural disasters (James, 2008; Rehman et al., 2019). For example, floods are considered one of the most serious natural disasters, especially to developing countries with inadequate flood preparedness and disaster management mechanisms. The recurring flooding phenomenon in Pakistan has caused hazardous impacts leading to heavy losses to human life, food resources and infrastructure (Qasim et al., 2016). A recent study by Rehman et al. (2019) has adopted a systems thinking approach, through the use of CLDs and Driver-Pressures-States-Impacts-Responses framework for key stakeholders to disaster risk reduction. A variety of social, institutional, cultural, infrastructural, technical and environmental factors leading to floods in Pakistan were analysed and interpreted using the systems tools. Policy recommendations for long-term flood disaster response, management and mitigation strategies, which also aim at facilitating resilience from floods for sustainable development, were suggested at various levels through the applications of systems thinking.

Systems thinking methodology and tools have also been adopted in other cases of global emergency and disaster events. The still on-going COVID-19 pandemic, which has presented unprecedented challenges to healthcare systems and human well-being, has attracted growing interests regarding the applications of systems thinking. Based on systems thinking principles, a new framework for systematically gathering people's pandemic experiences and reflecting on current crisis, as informed by revised critical systems heuristics, critical recovery and integral critical systems, has been proposed (Haley et al., 2021). The conceptual framework was designed to support a dialogic cultural or systemic approach to COVID-19, focusing on the creation of trusted public health information and development of effective communication of official health guidance to achieve resilience across diverse cultures from the COVID-19 pandemic.

Meanwhile, the case of Kerala was used as an illustrative example of innovations in the pandemic management of COVID-19 based on storytelling adopting systems thinking and casual loop modelling (Elias, 2021). A casual loop model consisting of six interacting feedback loops was developed, enabling visualisations of the interconnections among the major systems in relation to spread of COVID-19, communication innovations, effective public health, policy innovations, social innovations and technology innovations. This case study focusing on COVID-19 also provides valuable insights for future empirical studies regarding the applications of systems thinking in other pandemics. Furthermore, systems thinking has been largely advocated in formulating plans and interventions for resolving the complex social and health issues brought about by COVID-19 (Hassan et al., 2020). More research studies addressing health system resilience and recovery from the pandemic are critically needed for sustainable development.

Conclusion

A variety of studies have supported the versatile and promising applications of systems science in the healthcare discipline and strengthening of health systems. Case studies in different countries such as China and Canada also indicated the promising prospects of systems thinking to support sustainable healthcare systems. Considering the SDGs, and, in particular, SDG 3 which aims to ensure healthy lives and promote well-being for all at all ages, the potential of systems thinking for achieving the goals is highly rated. In this chapter, studies related to the use of systems thinking in the critical issues of health system resilience, healthy urban planning and education for a sustainable environment have been discussed. Circumstances such as the worldwide ageing population, increasing levels of pollution and more frequent occurrence of disaster events have all contributed to further serious loading of healthcare systems. Appropriate design and effective implementation of mitigation measures need to be based on a comprehensive perspective and a systemic approach to analyse the interconnections among different systems. Overall, more comprehensive studies regarding the applications of systems thinking approaches supported with systems tools such as CLDs and SOCME diagrams will be important for achieving a sustainable healthcare system and ultimately, a sustainable future.

References

Aghapour, A. H., Yazdani, M., Jolai, F., & Mojtahedi, M. (2019). Capacity planning and reconfiguration for disaster-resilient health infrastructure. *Journal of Building Engineering*, *26*, Article 100853. https://doi.org/10.1016/j.jobe.2019.100853

Agyepong, I. A., Aryeetey, G. C., Nonvignon, J., Asenso-Boadi, F., Dzikunu, H., Antwi, E., ... & Arhinful, D. K. (2014). Advancing the application of systems thinking in health: Provider payment and service supply behaviour and incentives in the Ghana National Health Insurance Scheme–a systems approach. *Health Research Policy and Systems*, *12*, Article 35. https://doi.org/10.1186/1478-4505-12-35

Bagnall, A. M., Radley, D., Jones, R., Gately, P., Nobles, J., Van Dijk, M., ... & Sahota, P. (2019). Whole systems approaches to obesity and other complex public health challenges: A systematic review. *BMC Public Health*, *19*, Article 8. https://doi.org/10.1186/s12889-018-6274-z

Best, A., Greenhalgh, T., Lewis, S., Saul, J. E., Carroll, S., & Bitz, J. (2012). Large-system transformation in health care: A realist review. *The Milbank Quarterly*, *90*(3), 421–456. https://doi.org/10.1111/j.1468-0009.2012.00670.x

Blanchet, K., & James, P. (2013). The role of social networks in the governance of health systems: The case of eye care systems in Ghana. *Health Policy and Planning*, *28*(2), 143–156. https://doi.org/10.1093/heapol/czs031

Blanchet, K., Nam, S. L., Ramalingam, B., & Pozo-Martin, F. (2017). Governance and capacity to manage resilience of health systems: Towards a new conceptual framework. *International Journal of Health Policy and Management*, *6*(8), 431–435. https://doi.org/10.15171/IJHPM.2017.36

Braithwaite, J., Zurynski, Y., Ludlow, K., Holt, J., Augustsson, H., & Campbell, M. (2019). Towards sustainable healthcare system performance in the 21st century in high-income countries: A protocol for a systematic review of the grey literature. *BMJ Open*, *9*(1), Article e025892. https://doi.org/10.1136/bmjopen-2018-025892

Brolan, C. E., McEwan, C. A., & Hill, P. S. (2019). Australia's overseas development aid commitment to health through the sustainable development goals: A multi-stakeholder perspective. *Globalization and Health*, *15*, Article 66. https://doi.org/10.1186/s12992-019-0507-5

Carey, G., Malbon, E., Carey, N., Joyce, A., Crammond, B., & Carey, A. (2015). Systems science and systems thinking for public health: A systematic review of the field. *BMJ Open*, *5*(12), Article e009002. https://doi.org/10.1136/bmjopen-2015-009002

Chiu, W. K. (2021). Pedagogy of emerging technologies in chemical education during the era of digitalization and artificial intelligence: A systematic review. *Education Sciences*, *11*(11), Article 709. https://doi.org/10.3390/educsci11110709

Chiu, W. K., & Fong, B. Y. F (2022). Chemical pollution and healthy ageing: The prominent need for a cleaner environment. In V. T. S. Law & B. Y. F. Fong

(Eds.), *Ageing with Dignity in Hong Kong and Asia. Quality of Life in Asia* (vol. 16). Springer, Singapore. https://doi.org/10.1007/978-981-19-3061-4_19

Chiu, W. K., Fong, B. Y. F., & Ho, W. Y. (2022). The importance of environmental sustainability for healthy ageing and the incorporation of systems thinking in education for a sustainable environment. *Asia Pacific Journal of Health Management, 17*(1), 84–89. https://doi.org/10.24083/apjhm.v17i1.1589

Chughtai, S., & Blanchet, K. (2017). Systems thinking in public health: A bibliographic contribution to a meta-narrative review. *Health Policy and Planning, 32*(4), 585–594. https://doi.org/10.1093/heapol/czw159

Constable, D. J., Jiménez-González, C., & Matlin, S. A. (2019). Navigating complexity using systems thinking in chemistry, with implications for chemistry education. *Journal of Chemical Education, 96*(12), 2689–2699. https://doi.org/10.1021/acs.jchemed.9b00368

Cristiano, S., & Zilio, S. (2021). Whose health in whose city? A systems thinking approach to support and evaluate plans, policies, and strategies for lasting urban health. *Sustainability, 13*(21), Article 12225. https://doi.org/10.3390/su132112225

De Savigny, D., & Adam, T. (Eds.). (2009). *Systems Thinking for Health Systems Strengthening*. World Health Organization. https://apo.who.int/publications/i/item/2009-11-13-systems-thinking-for-health-systems-strengthening

Dugan, K. E., Mosyjowski, E. A., Daly, S. R., & Lattuca, L. R. (2021). Systems thinking assessments in engineering: A systematic literature review. *Systems Research and Behavioral Science, 39*(4), 840–866. https://doi.org/10.1002/sres.2808

Elias, A. A. (2021). Kerala's innovations and flexibility for Covid-19 recovery: Storytelling using systems thinking. *Global Journal of Flexible Systems Management, 22*(1), 33–43. https://doi.org/10.1007/s40171-021-00268-8

Folke, C., Carpenter, S. R., Walker, B., Scheffer, M., Chapin, T., & Rockström, J. (2010). Resilience thinking: Integrating resilience, adaptability and transformability. *Ecology and Society, 15*(4). Article 20. http://www.ecologyandsociety.org/vol15/iss4/art20/

Fong, B. Y. F., Chiu, W. K., Chan, W. F., & Lam, T. Y. (2021). A review study of a green diet and healthy ageing. *International Journal of Environmental Research and Public Health, 18*(15), Article 8024. https://doi.org/10.3390/ijerph18158024

Fowler, W. C., Ting, J. M., Meng, S., Li, L., & Tirrell, M. V. (2019). Integrating systems thinking into teaching emerging technologies. *Journal of Chemical Education, 96*(12), 2805–2813. https://doi.org/10.1021/acs.jchemed.9b00280

Guo, H., Qiao, W., & Liu, J. (2019). Dynamic feedback analysis of influencing factors of existing building energy-saving renovation market based on system dynamics in China. *Sustainability, 11*(1), Article 273. https://doi.org/10.3390/su11010273

Haley, D., Paucar-Caceres, A., & Schlindwein, S. (2021). A critical inquiry into the value of systems thinking in the time of COVID-19 crisis. *Systems, 9*(1), Article 13. https://doi.org/10.3390/systems9010013

Hassan, I., Obaid, F., Ahmed, R., Abdelrahman, L., Adam, S., Adam, O., ... & Kashif, T. (2020). A systems thinking approach for responding to the COVID-19 pandemic. *Eastern Mediterranean Health Journal, 26*(8), 872–876. https://doi.org/10.26719/emhj.20.090

Hill, P. S. (2011). Understanding global health governance as a complex adaptive system. *Global Public Health, 6*(6), 593–605. https://doi.org/10.1080/17441691003762108

Holland, J. H. (2006). Studying complex adaptive systems. *Journal of Systems Science and Complexity, 19*, 1–8. https://doi.org/10.1007/s11424-006-0001-z

Holme, T. (2020). Using the chemistry of pharmaceuticals to introduce sustainable chemistry and systems thinking in general chemistry. *Sustainable Chemistry and Pharmacy, 16*, Article 100234. https://doi.org/10.1016/j.scp.2020.100234

Hossain, N. U. I., Dayarathna, V. L., Nagahi, M., & Jaradat, R. (2020). Systems thinking: A review and bibliometric analysis. *Systems, 8*(3), Article 23. https://doi.org/10.3390/systems8030023

Hurst, G. A. (2020). Systems thinking approaches for international green chemistry education. *Current Opinion in Green and Sustainable Chemistry, 21*, 93–97. https://doi.org/10.1016/j.cogsc.2020.02.004

Hussain, S., Javadi, D., Andrey, J., Ghaffar, A., & Labonté, R. (2020). Health intersectoralism in the sustainable development goal era: From theory to practice. *Globalization and Health, 16*, Article 15. https://doi.org/10.1186/s12992-020-0543-1

James, E. (2008). Getting ahead of the next disaster: Recent preparedness efforts in Indonesia. *Development in Practice, 18*(3), 424–429. https://doi.org/10.1080/09614520802030607

Kümmerer, K., Clark, J. H., & Zuin, V. G. (2020). Rethinking chemistry for a circular economy. *Science, 367*(6476), 369–370. https://doi.org/10.1126/science.aba4979

Kutzin, J., & Sparkes, S. P. (2016). Health systems strengthening, universal health coverage, health security and resilience. *Bulletin of the World Health Organization, 94*(1), 2. https://doi.org/10.2471/BLT.15.165050

Lagarda-Leyva, E. A., & Ruiz, A. (2019). A systems thinking model to support long-term bearability of the healthcare system: The case of the Province of Quebec. *Sustainability, 11*(24), Article 7028. https://doi.org/10.3390/su11247028

Leischow, S. J., & Milstein, B. (2006). Systems thinking and modeling for public health practice. *American Journal of Public Health, 96*(3), 403–405. https://doi.org/10.2105/AJPH.2005.082842

Litaker, D., Tomolo, A., Liberatore, V., Stange, K. C., & Aron, D. (2006). Using complexity theory to build interventions that improve health care delivery in primary care. *Journal of General Internal Medicine, 21*(2), S30–S34. https://doi.org/10.1007/s11606-006-0272-z

Luke, J., Franklin, R., Aitken, P., & Dyson, J. (2021). Safer hospital infrastructure assessments for socio-natural disaster–A scoping review. *Prehospital and Disaster Medicine, 36*(5), 627–635. https://doi.org/10.1017/S1049023X21000650

Mahaffy, P. G., Matlin, S. A., Holme, T. A., & MacKellar, J. (2019b). Systems thinking for education about the molecular basis of sustainability. *Nature Sustainability, 2*(5), 362–370. https://doi.org/10.1038/s41893-019-0285-3

Mahaffy, P. G., Matlin, S. A., Whalen, J. M., & Holme, T. A. (2019a). Integrating the molecular basis of sustainability into general chemistry through systems thinking. *Journal of Chemical Education, 96*(12), 2730–2741. https://doi.org/10.1021/acs.jchemed.9b00390

Matlin, S. A., Mehta, G., Hopf, H., & Krief, A. (2015). The role of chemistry in inventing a sustainable future. *Nature Chemistry, 7*(12), 941–943. https://doi.org/10.1038/nchem.2389

Mavhura, E. (2017). Applying a systems-thinking approach to community resilience analysis using rural livelihoods: The case of Muzarabani district, Zimbabwe. *International Journal of Disaster Risk Reduction, 25*, 248–258. https://doi.org/10.1016/j.ijdrr.2017.09.008

Mayunga, J. S. (2007). Understanding and applying the concept of community disaster resilience: A capital-based approach. *Summer Academy for Social Vulnerability and Resilience Building, 1*(1), 1–16.

Minyard, K. J., Ferencik, R., Ann Phillips, M., & Soderquist, C. (2014). Using systems thinking in state health policymaking: An educational initiative. *Health Systems, 3*(2), 117–123. https://doi.org/10.1057/hs.2013.17

Munday, D. F., Johnson, S. A., & Griffiths, F. E. (2003). Complexity theory and palliative care. *Palliative Medicine, 17*(4), 308–309. https://doi.org/10.1191/0269216303pm771oa

Orgill, M., York, S., & MacKellar, J. (2019). Introduction to systems thinking for the chemistry education community. *Journal of Chemical Education, 96*(12), 2720–2729. https://doi.org/10.1021/acs.jchemed.9b00169

Peters, D. H. (2014). The application of systems thinking in health: Why use systems thinking?. *Health Research Policy and Systems, 12*, Article 51. https://doi.org/10.1186/1478-4505-12-51

Pype, P., Mertens, F., Helewaut, F., & Krystallidou, D. (2018). Healthcare teams as complex adaptive systems: Understanding team behaviour through team members' perception of interpersonal interaction. *BMC Health Services Research, 18*, Article 570. https://doi.org/10.1186/s12913-018-3392-3

Qasim, S., Qasim, M., Shrestha, R. P., Khan, A. N., Tun, K., & Ashraf, M. (2016). Community resilience to flood hazards in Khyber Pukhthunkhwa province of Pakistan. *International Journal of Disaster Risk Reduction, 18*, 100–106. https://doi.org/10.1016/j.ijdrr.2016.03.009

Rehman, J., Sohaib, O., Asif, M., & Pradhan, B. (2019). Applying systems thinking to flood disaster management for a sustainable development. *International Journal of Disaster Risk Reduction, 36*, Article 101101. https://doi.org/10.1016/j.ijdrr.2019.101101

Reynolds, M., Blackmore, C., Ison, R., Shah, R., & Wedlock, E. (2018). The role of systems thinking in the practice of implementing sustainable development goals. In W. Leal Filho (Ed.), *Handbook of Sustainability Science and Research* (pp. 677–698). *World Sustainability Series*. Springer, Cham. https://doi.org/10.1007/978-3-319-63007-6_42

Rutter, H., Savona, N., Glonti, K., Bibby, J., Cummins, S., Finegood, D. T.,... & White, M. (2017). The need for a complex systems model of evidence for public health. *The Lancet*, *390*(10112), 2602–2604. https://doi.org/10.1016/S0140-6736(17)31267-9

Rwashana, A. S., Nakubulwa, S., Nakakeeto-Kijjambu, M., & Adam, T. (2014). Advancing the application of systems thinking in health: Understanding the dynamics of neonatal mortality in Uganda. *Health Research Policy and Systems*, *12*, Article 36. https://doi.org/10.1186/1478-4505-12-36

Sarriot, E. G., Kouletio, M., Jahan, S., Rasul, I., & Musha, A. K. M. (2014). Advancing the application of systems thinking in health: Sustainability evaluation as learning and sense-making in a complex urban health system in Northern Bangladesh. *Health Research Policy and Systems*, *12*, Article 45. https://doi.org/10.1186/1478-4505-12-45

Schultz, M., Lai, J., Ferguson, J. P., & Delaney, S. (2021). Topics amenable to a systems thinking approach: Secondary and tertiary perspectives. *Journal of Chemical Education*, *98*(10), 3100–3109. https://doi.org/10.1021/acs.jchemed.1c00203

Simoni, M., Baldacci, S., Maio, S., Cerrai, S., Sarno, G., & Viegi, G. (2015). Adverse effects of outdoor pollution in the elderly. *Journal of Thoracic Disease*, *7*(1), 34–45. https://doi.org/10.3978/j.issn.2072-1439.2014.12.10

Tan, J., Wen, H. J., & Awad, N. (2005). Health care and services delivery systems as complex adaptive systems. *Communications of the ACM*, *48*(5), 36–44. https://doi.org/10.1145/1060710.1060737

Van der Brugge, R., & Van Raak, R. (2007). Facing the adaptive management challenge: Insights from transition management. *Ecology and Society*, *12*(2), Article 33. https://doi.org/10.5751/ES-02227-120233

Wang, X., Wang, H., & Zhang, C. (2022). A literature review of social commerce research from a systems thinking perspective. *Systems*, *10*(3), Article 56. https://doi.org/10.3390/systems10030056

Wissinger, J. E., Visa, A., Saha, B. B., Matlin, S. A., Mahaffy, P. G., Kümmerer, K., & Cornell, S. (2021). Integrating Sustainability into Learning in Chemistry. *Journal of Chemical Education*, *98*(4), 1061–1063. https://doi.org/10.1021/acs.jchemed.1c00284

Xiao, Y., Zhao, K., Bishai, D. M., & Peters, D. H. (2013). Essential drugs policy in three rural counties in China: What does a complexity lens add?. *Social Science & Medicine*, *93*, 220–228. https://doi.org/10.1016/j.socscimed.2012.09.034

Zhang, X., Bloom, G., Xu, X., Chen, L., Liang, X., & Wolcott, S. J. (2014). Advancing the application of systems thinking in health: Managing rural China health system development in complex and dynamic contexts. *Health Research Policy and Systems, 12*(1), Article 44. https://doi.org/10.1186/1478-4505-12-44

Zimmerman, J. B., Anastas, P. T., Erythropel, H. C., & Leitner, W. (2020). Designing for a green chemistry future. *Science, 367*(6476), 397–400. https://doi.org/10.1126/science.aay3060

Zuin, V. G., Eilks, I., Elschami, M., & Kümmerer, K. (2021). Education in green chemistry and in sustainable chemistry: Perspectives towards sustainability. *Green Chemistry, 23*(4), 1594–1608. https://doi.org/10.1039/D0GC03313H

2 Impacts of Sustainable Development Goal 3 and Health Systems

Ben Y. F. Fong

Introduction

The Sustainable Development Goals (SDGs) proposed by the United Nations (UN) (https://sdgs.un.org/goals) were passed by all UN Member States in 2015 to act as a shared blueprint for peace and prosperity for mankind and the globe, and to attend to challenges on earth such as poverty, well-being and equality. There are 17 goals, each carries specific targets with objectives to achieve a better and sustainable future in the related thematic issues in all aspects of life and daily living, including water, energy, climate, oceans, urbanisation, transport, science and technology.

SDG 3 seeks to ensure health and well-being for all people at every stage of life. This SDG focuses major health-related issues and needs of life, including reproductive, maternal and child health; communicable, non-communicable and environmental diseases; universal health coverage (UHC); and access to safe, effective, quality and affordable medicines and vaccines for all people in the world. It also advocates increase in input and resources in research and development, financing healthcare programmes, and building strong capacity by all nations and regions in the context of reduction and management of health risks, but the 2020 COVID-19 pandemic is devastating most health systems in the world and threatens the good health outcomes already attained by many countries and cities.

Impacts of SDG 3 in Community Healthcare Delivery

The Sustainable Development Goal 3: 'Ensure healthy lives and promote well-being for all at all ages' is broad, but in essence, SDG 3 carries a very strong and prominent message of UHC (World Health Organization, n.d.a). The WHO has been advocating UHC in its

DOI: 10.4324/9781003305637-2

primary care initiative for decades in the context of human right and right to healthcare in all societies, irrespective of financial background or ethnicity. In this context, the access to quality healthcare by the population is a very essential outcome in all health systems that must be achieved in the context of the SDG 3 health goal. No one in the entire community should be left behind. In striking towards UHC and healthcare equity, other related SDGs and public health services, such as decrease in poverty, gender equality, clean and safe drinking water, environmental sanitation, sustainable forms of energy, safe and healthy cities, food and nutrition and education, are equally important and should be taken into consideration by the governments and healthcare professions (World Health Organization, 2017). These interwoven SDGs include SDG 1 (Poverty), SDG 2 (Zero Hunger), SDG 4 (Quality Education), SDG 5 (Gender Equality), SDG 6 (Clean Water and Sanitation), SDG 13 (Climate Action), SDG 14 (Life under Water), SDG 15 (Life on Land) and SDG 17 (Partnerships for Goals). The sudden occurrence of COVID-19 pandemic in March 2020 had been consuming enormous resources in the world and there were obvious unfavourable effects on the progress and unexpected negative setbacks in economic productivity and human development. The health systems of most countries and societies have been grossly overwhelmed, even in the brink of collapse (Khetrapal & Bhatia, 2020; World Economic Forum, 2020).

The SDG 3 Targets

3.1 *By 2030, reduce the global maternal mortality ratio to less than 70 per 100,000 live births*

Before the pandemic, it was noted that significant progress had been made, for instance, in the reduction of preventable maternal and infant deaths, increase in childhood immunisation and better access to reproductive healthcare. Maternal mortality ratio fell by 2.9% annually in the years from 2000 to 2017, a total of 38% during this period. However, a decline level of 6.4% each year would be adequate to meeting the target (World Economic Forum, 2020).

3.2 *By 2030, end preventable deaths of newborns and children under five years of age, with all countries aiming to reduce neonatal mortality to at least as low as 12 per 1,000 live births and under-5 mortality to at least as low as 25 per 1,000 live births*

Most of deaths in the newborn babies arise from three preventable and potentially treatable conditions, namely complications from prematurity, intrapartum-related deaths and infections at this age of new life. Therefore, resources should be allocated in the care during the periods of pregnancy, childbirth and the first month of infancy to help and save more mothers and newborns, avoid the chance of stillbirths and reduce the consequent disabilities among them. Such public strategy help to ascertain optimal development of the children as well as lifelong health and well-being. In addition, the role of quality of care in health services is also evident and should be the right of every pregnant woman and child. This objective requires the healthcare systems to provide quality medicines and commodities that are essential, to exercise clinical interventions and practices which are evidence-based, equitable and humanistic, and to ensure prevention and control of infections, all supported by qualified, competent and highly motivated staff, as well as the use of accurate and timely information in service delivery (World Health Organization, 2020). In essence, the systems should aim to achieve UHC for equity and quality care, and to end preventable deaths. There should also be attention to human rights, gender and equality. In addition, appropriate measures in environment and nutrition are conducive to healthier lives in building resilient and sustainable health systems (Foreign, Commonwealth & Development Office, Government of United Kingdom, 2021).

3.3 *By 2030, end the epidemics of AIDS, tuberculosis, malaria and neglected tropical diseases and combat hepatitis, water-borne diseases and other communicable diseases*

According to the World Health Organization (n.d.b), there were 1.7 million people newly infected by HIV in 2019, and 299 million malaria cases worldwide in the same year. A 2% of reduction in the incidence of tuberculosis (TB) was recorded every year between 2015 and 2019. The WHO had formulated a global strategy on HIV in five directions for the period of 2016–2021 to guide priority actions by countries and regions affected by the infection. The directives are (i) focused action with accurate information, (ii) impact through interventions, (iii) equitable delivery of care and services, (iv) financial sustainability and (v) innovation for acceleration. For the control of TB, reduction in the number of TB deaths by 90% and a reduction in the TB incidence rate by 80% were the targets. Strategies for the control and elimination of malaria are targeted at reducing case incidence and mortality rates of malaria, eliminating the infection and preventing a resurgence of malaria in all countries (World Health Organization, n.d.b). With the onset of the COVID-19 pandemic, all countries find it difficult to maintain attention to other epidemics and infectious diseases at the same time but there is an urgent need to care for and to mitigate negative impacts of the pandemic to the most vulnerable groups in all nations and cities.

3.4 *By 2030, reduce by one third premature mortality from non-communicable diseases through prevention and treatment and promote mental health and well-being*

The Global Action Plan for the Prevention and Control of Non-communicable diseases (NCDs) (2013–2020) of the WHO is embedded with this target (3.4), and it includes options and recommendations for control of risk factors, enhanced disease management in primary healthcare, surveillance of NCDs and health promotion activities. A life course approach is adopted in the implementation of the global action plan, with reference to the working principles of human rights, UHC and equity. NCDs account for majority of the disease burden in most populations. They affect life expectancy and quality of life of individuals and their family members and carers. Early management of NCDs is not only more feasible, but is much less expensive to the society and individuals. This care option can be readily taken up in primary healthcare, resulting in the reduction of morbidity and premature mortality, and hence improvement in the quality of life (Varghese, 2017). However, many governments do not provide adequate health dollars in support of health promotion and disease prevention, despite it is known that the costs of treatment are high and expected to grow fairly fast, particularly with an increasing ageing population in the world. This is translated into a serious burden on all healthcare systems (European Commission, n.d.). In the promotion of mental health and wellness, an interventional framework at multiple levels to decrease unnecessary mortality in people suffering from severe mental disorders (SMDs) has been proposed. It has a focus on the four common risk factors, which are the use of tobacco, harmful consumption of alcohol, unhealthy eating habits and physical inactivity. There is also an attention to the impact of relevant health interventions in the population to ameliorate the risk factors, such as taxation on cigarettes and spirits, and restricted access to these substances. A tailored approach in the care of people with SMDs is necessary, in terms of improving the cognitive capacity of sufferers, and building the capacity of providers, carers and family members. Mental health services should be supported with clinical skills and medicines applied in the care of NCDs, and they should be included in the medical records of patients affected by SMDs and NCDs. It is also recommended to adopt an integrative approach with appropriate management interventions by healthcare providers. In essence, the integrative care for people with SMDs requires a systematic and sustained thinking at various levels of the healthcare system. For instance, national or local programmes for specific NCDs, mental health and primary care services should jointly develop operational guidance and allocate optimal resources for implementation of appropriate strategies and action plans in these areas to achieve this target (3.4; Varghese, 2017).

3.5 *Strengthen the prevention and treatment of substance abuse, including narcotic drug abuse and harmful use of alcohol*

In 2017, the Forum on Alcohol, Drugs & Addictive Behaviours organised by the WHO Department of Mental Health and Substance Abuse signified the interest and commitment to address the harmful consumption of alcohol. It pointed out that the reduction in alcohol consumption as a priority was critical in combating NCDs burden and achieving SDGs, particularly target 3.4. After all, alcohol is widely known to have short-term and lifelong social and health harms to people, and is an effect modifier of risk factors to the health of individuals, irrespective of the level of consumption. Such issues should be considered in policy development in the prevention and management of alcohol abuse by government departments, in a similar approach when dealing with unhealthy diet and tobacco use. These are challenges to implementation of effective alcohol control policies. An internationally binding legal instrument has been proposed to curb the harmful use of alcohol. A joint effort through coordination and collaboration of health agencies, with the input of expert advice, is needed (NCD Alliance, 2017).

3.6 *By 2030, halve the number of global deaths and injuries from road traffic accidents*

In September 2015, the United Nations General Assembly adopted the global sustainable development goals for road safety to reduce the number of deaths and injuries from road traffic accidents. In this connection, safe, affordable, accessible and sustainable transport systems should be available to everyone. Public transport is specifically emphasised for the particular needs of vulnerable residents, including women, children, older adults and people with disabilities. Later on, in August 2020, the UN General Assembly suggested to include policies and measures for better post-crash care, frameworks of enhanced driver qualification, legislation on use of seatbelt, child restraints, alcohol and drug driving and new technologies for vehicle safety. They also called for limitation of speeds to 30 km/h in high density community areas. Road safety has always been a concern for the Australians. In 2012, they developed a voluntarily adopted tool, ISO 39001, which was the first road traffic safety management standard to help organisations to include the Safe System approach in routine operations. The Australian government is committed to collaborate with international forums and organisations in global efforts to improve road safety. There are international exchanges of knowledge and expertise through the Asia Pacific Economic Cooperation (APEC), the World Road Association, the Organization for Economic Cooperation and Development (OECD) and the International Transport Forum and the Global Road Safety Facility. The Australian Department of Infrastructure, Transport Regional Development, Communications and the Arts also funds the annual Australasian Road Safety Conference and provides sponsorship for delegates from low- and middle-income countries in Asia-Pacific and Africa (National Road Safety Strategy, n.d.).

3.7 *By 2030, ensure universal access to sexual and reproductive healthcare services, including for family planning, information and education and the integration of reproductive health into national strategies and programmes*

Studies have found some obvious progress in sexual and reproductive healthcare services (SRHS), while there are challenges to reach the targets. Access to SRHS is still limited, particularly in developing countries. A life course approach is incorporated in a comprehensive SRHS package forming part of primary healthcare services, in which there are adequate referrals to ensure universal coverage of SRHS. However, the quality and utilisation of services are considered unsatisfactory and noted to be causative factors leading to mortality. In Thailand, while universal access to quality SRHS is assured by the government through the health benefits package, there are high adolescent birth rate and inadequate coverage of HPV vaccination for school girls. The needs of family planning for young adolescents are not met and compounded by gaps in comprehensive sex education for this age group. As a remedial measure, the coverage of HPV vaccine will be enhanced by its availability and provision. In addition, cervical cancer screening coverage is far from meeting the target in Thailand because of the lack of awareness and knowledge, cultural beliefs among the people and shortage of professional support (Panichkriangkrai et al., 2020). In another context, a Chinese study has noted the problem of high abortion rates arising from the perverse financial incentives for healthcare organisations, and it draws urgent policy consideration of SRHS and comprehensive sex education to conform to the context in the country, particularly concerning adolescent women (Fang et al., 2020). SDG 5 on gender equality and empowerment of all women and girls is related to this target (3.7) (Panichkriangkrai et al., 2020).

3.8 *Achieve universal health coverage, including financial risk protection, access to quality essential healthcare services and access to safe, effective, quality and affordable essential medicines and vaccines for all*

UHC is always the top priority agenda of the World Health Organization when 'Health for All by the Year 2000' in the Alma Ata Declaration of 1978 was formulated. Thus, this target (3.8) is widely considered as the most important and the leading directive among all health-related SDGs. The Declaration was strongly advocating primary healthcare as the essential care made universally accessible to cater for the needs of all individuals in the community, through integrating care, prevention, promotion and education in health systems. Primary healthcare is based on clinical practice which is practical, scientifically sound and socially acceptable and appropriate technology. It aims to improve population health, and upgrade the performance and effectiveness of health systems by optimising overall health expenditure. Primary healthcare also ensures access to essential health services and medicines and vaccines for all people. Health systems must strengthen primary healthcare and attain UHC and equity to align with the global health policy initiatives (van Weel & Kidd, 2018). This is far more important for developing countries where access to affordable, quality, safe and essential medicines and vaccines is not a matter of fact. Learning from the two-plus-year-long COVID-19 pandemic, all countries should be committed work together to optimise research and access to innovative health technologies in the high-quality production of medicines, vaccines and diagnostics, supported by innovative service delivery at affordable prices to the needy people. Notwithstanding such a proposition, 19.4 million children in the world did not receive diphtheria-tetanus-pertussis or measles vaccines in 2018 though some promising coverage of childhood immunisation had been noted (World Economic Forum, 2020). Governments and the healthcare professionals still have a lot to do to achieve the target, despite the Doha Declaration of 2002 on the Agreement on Trade Related Aspects of Intellectual Property Rights Agreement and Public Health, which affirmed the protection of public health in developing countries, and access to medicines for all (World Health Organization, 2002).

3.9 *By 2030, substantially reduce the number of deaths and illnesses from hazardous chemicals and air, water and soil pollution and contamination*

The right to health also entails environmental and other human rights for a conducive environment to live and work with the aim to achieve the SDGs. Pollution is among the top drivers of loss biodiversity on earth, jeopardising the ability of ecosystems to provide clean air, uncontaminated water and safe food to mankind. The global situation is worsened by climate change which is drawing more and more world attention in recent years (Kupka, 2021). Deteriorated and degraded environment accounts for over one fifth of all deaths in the world. For example, over a million lives are lost every year arising from the exposures to the many more chemicals every day, mostly are preventable, and 193,000 deaths are likely caused by unintentional poisonings. However, only about half of the countries have poisons centres. In a sense, pollution and contamination of air, water and soil in the environment has a negative implication to human rights, life, health, water and food and gender equality, in the context of sustainability for people and the habitats in the world and generations in the future eras. To achieve this target (3.9), a number of proactive actions are essential in the long run on related areas and necessities of human activities, concerning the global terrestrial ecosystems (Goal 15), oceans (Goal 14), cities (Goal 11), water and sanitation (Goal 6), energy (Goal 7), climate change (Goal 13), consumption and production patterns (Goal 12) as well as on equality (Goal 10), gender equality (Goal 5), education (Goal 4), peace, justice and strong institutions (Goal 16), as well as partnerships, technology and finance (Goal 17). Social and economic factors such as age, gender, socioeconomic status, education, occupation, income, housing and ethnicity are contributing, both directly and indirectly, to the conditions of environment, thus affecting the morbidity and mortality of the populations on earth. It is disquieting to see the 3.5 billion poorest people of the world relying directly on the environment for their basic needs of daily living, such as water, food and shelter (UN Environment, 2017).

In the perspectives of policy and law enforcement, management of water resources, chemicals and waste must be among the top priorities of all governments, and environmental health and protection authorities. Kupka (2021) has recommended a science-policy panel on chemicals, wastes and pollution to incorporate the best science in making policies and designing solutions and to involve stakeholders in the government, private sector, academia and wider population. Some countries have official organisations and strategies concerning such management in the legislation, imports and exports, standards and registration of chemical products, occupational exposure limits and emergency and contingency plans. In 2017, legally binding controls on lead content in paint were noted in 65 countries. Nonetheless, a great challenge is noted in the implementation, compliance and enforcement of the government instruments in the control and management of chemicals and environment, often arising from some intrinsic and structural limitations in institutional capacity, coordination within the government, access to information and materials related to law enforcement, particularly in developing countries. However, voluntary, non-government organisations and some global alliances are found to be instrumental in motivating stakeholder in pushing for improvement and actions in environmental improvements like in the use of fuels and clean air quality (UN Environment, 2017). Sound and appropriate public policy concerning pollution, contamination and environment issues should be based on the latest and best available scientific knowledge and evidence. Intervention strategies are thus more effective in implementation to achieve the SDGs and to safeguard the rights of people.

3.a *Strengthen the implementation of the World Health Organization Framework Convention on Tobacco Control in all countries, as appropriate*

The WHO Framework Convention on Tobacco Control (FCTC) aims to encourage tobacco control policies based on evidence in all countries. Global consumption of cigarettes has been decreasing in the past decades, but the rate of reduction has not been enhanced by the adoption of the FCTC. There was a reversed trend in the low income countries. Little difference has been noted in the low- and middle-income countries that cigarette consumption of their residents was matching that of high-income countries. Moreover, there are problems in the acknowledgement of treaties, obligations and capacity of governments to implement the recommendations (Hoffman et al., 2019). Hence, this target

(3.a) must be adopted by all governments in the world in the fight against tobacco use in the community, particularly among children and young people.

3.b *Substantially increase health financing and the recruitment, development, training and retention of the health workforce in developing countries, especially in least developed countries and small island developing States*

This target (3.b) is well discussed and illustrated in Chapter 4, *"Development of Healthcare Professionals and Leadership in Achieving Sustainability"*, particularly in the sections of 'Recruiting Foreign-Trained Healthcare Professionals' and 'Professional Substitution'.

3.c *Strengthen the capacity of all countries, in particular, developing countries, for early warning, risk reduction and management of national and global health risks*

Natural and man-made accidents and disasters, including climate-related disasters like typhoons, hurricanes, tsunamis, landslides, flooding, bush fires, collapsed buildings, nuclear plant accidents, etc., have cost enormous loss of lives and properties as much as genetic and behavioural health risks. The impacts in the social, economic and environmental perspectives ultimately affect the sustainable development, particularly in countries and regions with limited or underdeveloped resources for early warning, and reduction and management of the risks. For instance, some island nations would have the entire country devastated by a hurricane. The public health crisis of COVID-19 pandemic is by far the worst known global disaster caused by an emerging novel virus that has put the world to a 'once-in-a-lifetime' test of the health and disaster response systems. It has exposed the seemingly gross unpreparedness and the lack of capacity in many countries and regions of both developed and developing economies, all of which are badly and unexpectedly affected. [At the time of writing], the pandemic is far from over. All nations are learning a great lesson from the painful experience in emergency responses and disaster management involving all government departments and stakeholders from virtually the entire population. Capacity of all countries must be strengthened to deal with the complexity of this kind and similar health-related disaster and the challenging changes that are not predictable even by the best model, artificial intelligence and experts. There must be a paradigm shift to avoid similar events from happening. Innovative and integrated approaches such as systems thinking and sustainable development strategy are suggested in building powerful long-term resilience into system operations, supported by co-ordination of everyone in the community (Bello et al., 2021).

Framework for Action for Strengthening Health Systems to Improve Health Outcomes

The primary aim of this Framework for Action is to clarify and strengthen the role of WHO in health systems to give effective support to member states and partners in this area in a fast changing world and

> to promote a common understanding of what a health system is and what constitutes health systems strengthening. It also provides a basis to support countries in scaling up health systems and services: addressing bottlenecks in a collaborative, coordinated way, driven by desired health outcomes, to achieve sustainable system-wide effects. To be most effective, this process must be country-led, based on priorities set out in comprehensive national health plans.
>
> (World Health Organization, 2007)

The Framework emphasises the notion that health is 'everyone's business', and this is embedded in the constitution of WHO and the basic principles of primary healthcare. In the developing world, health outcomes and equality are poor and low. It is undesirable and unacceptable because affordable new technologies can help to prevent and reduce much of the disease burden in these countries and regions, where availability of drugs, vaccines, health information about care and prevention is in question and is often non-timely, and, worse still, unreliable, of insufficient quality and of unreasonable cost to the users. Health systems in the developing economies are considered as inadequate or even collapsing, constituting barriers to the adoption of international guidelines such as the Millennium Development Goals for best practices (United Nations Development Program, 2008).

Derived from the World health report 2000, the WHO Framework describe the six "building blocks" that constitute health system. The building blocks are 'service delivery; health workforce; information; medical products, vaccines and technologies; financing; and leadership and governance (stewardship)'. The blocks should be considered in an integrated approach, appreciating the inter-dependence of all the blocks in building the power of interventions and improving the performance of health systems comprehensively and adequately, resulting in measurable impact on health outcomes. The Framework supports policymakers and practitioners in addressing problems and issues of health systems and care delivery, such as financial and physical accessibility, health facilities, knowledge, skills, performance and motivation of providers, leadership and management competence, interdisciplinary and cross-sectoral partnership and collaboration and public accountability (United Nations Development Program, 2008).

Sustainable Healthcare Services and Delivery

To achieve sustainability of health systems, the services and their delivery should conform to standards and measurements of accessibility, coverage, quality and safety in the context of population health. Systems oriented to primary healthcare are in the better position in such endeavours for countries and regions, particularly in the developing world. Commitment of governments to achieving the health-related sustainable development goals, as noted in the 2018 Declaration of Astana, is just the beginning. There should be health in all policies (HiAP) to set the structure, process and outcomes for a functioning health system in service delivery, cross-sectoral partnership and community empowerment.

Taking a primary healthcare as an example in the perspective of systems thinking and building blocks of health systems, it is generally agreed that achievement of SDGs does not happen by service delivery alone. There must be sufficient well-educated, qualified, experienced and courteous healthcare professionals and supporting staff to provide appropriate care and services to the community in an effective and professional manner. There should be continuing competency-based education, with emphasis on ethics, and respectful and quality care, for best practices. Shortage of health workers is an international issue affecting many nations, as well as the geographic maldistribution and continuing wastage (Refer to Chapter 4). At the same time adequate and sustaining funding sources are fundamental to support the system in meeting the needs of the population and the relevant SDG targets. Government expenditure on health is always essential and crucial in steering the service provisions, technological advances and application and performance of the system. Accurate, timely and trustworthy information steers professional services, particularly during emergencies, and affects the understanding, and hence, the health seeking behaviours of the public. These information-driven care is translated to the outcomes of service delivery and the resilience of the system in normal time and during expected events.

Health literacy in the community or sectors of it must be strengthened through lifelong health education in schools, the society and workplaces (Chotchoungchatchai et al., 2020).

The entire world has been fully engaged in combating the COVID-19 pandemic since the beginning of 2020. Some health systems were in the brink of collapse when encountering thousands of affected cases and subsequent deaths. Many governments were caught un- or under-prepared for outbreaks of such a magnitude, causing almost 600 million confirmed cases (7.5% of the world population) and over 6 million deaths as of 26 August 2022. Much has been said about leadership and governance in the responsible government portfolios in the responses and precautious measures, including lockdown decisions and border control. While nothing is absolutely right or wrong, nobody has the crystal ball to foresee the extremely unpredictable behaviour and mutation of the virus. Unfortunately, officials have been 'removed' from their posts for poor performance or 'incorrect' directions in some countries. Led by forward-thinking leaders, revamped preparedness, linked with relevant SDGs, through field experience, evidence and new knowledge, untoward mistakes, objective assessment and expert opinion, should help to damper the impacts of the pandemic on all nations and strengthen sustainable health systems during normal time. More financial input to re-invent and reinvigorate health systems for sustainable health services with the objectives to improve access, quality and safety of health system has been advocated, learning from the experience of the pandemic. Eventually healthy lifestyles among residents count for any community on earth (Khetrapal & Bhatia, 2020).

Quality is imperative to sustainable healthcare services in maximising outputs and optimising user satisfaction. Commitment at all levels of the system is required, but usually not natural. Quality management should address issues up stream and attend to the possible process defects or deficiency even at the planning stage. Systemic process issues are fixed to prevent errors (Fong, 2019). Leaders and top managers of health systems must possess such a vision and conviction in assurance of quality through evidence-based strategies, strict regulations, conducive workplace practices and continuous education in the system. Initiatives must be disseminated throughout the systems in a sound and encouraging manner to build a momentum for implementation. High-quality and accountable health systems are desirable in the achievement of SDGs (Kruk et al., 2018). SDG 3 recommends improvement of health outcomes through equity or UHC, accessible and affordable services, reduction of mortality, disease prevention, avoidance of epidemics in stable ecosystems and robust environments for reliable and timely delivery of quality care to the community. A global effort of unconditional collaboration involving all nations with the aim to achieve the targets of SDGs is beneficial to mankind when the world is facing with disastrous consequences from the pandemic, wars, natural disasters, major accidents, economic depression and international tension. No nation should be left behind in the pursuit of SDGs and better life (Cerf, 2019).

References

Bello, O., Bustamante, A., & Pizarro, P. (2021). *Planning for disaster risk reduction within the framework of the 2030 agenda for sustainable development.* United Nations publication: Santiago. https://repositorio.cepal.org/bitstream/handle/11362/46639/1/S2000452_en.pdf

Chotchoungchatchai, S., Marshall, A. I., Witthayapipopsakul, W., Panichkriangkrai, W., Patcharanarumol, W., & Tangcharoensathien, V. (2020). Primary health care and sustainable development goals. *Bulletin of the World Health Organization, 98*(11), 792–800. https://doi.org/10.2471/BLT.19.245613

Cerf, M. E. (2019). Sustainable development goal integration, interdependence, and implementation: The environment–economic–health nexus and universal health coverage. *Global Challenges, 3*(9), Article 1900021. https://doi.org/10.1002/gch2.201900021

European Commission. (n.d.). *EU non-communicable diseases (NCDs) initiative.* https://health.ec.europa.eu/system/files/2022-04/ncd_initiative_faq_en.pdf

Fang, J., Tang, S., Tan, X., & Tolhurst, J. (2020). Achieving SDG related sexual and reproductive health targets in China: What are appropriate indicators and how we interpret them? *Reproductive Health, 17,* Article 84. https://doi.org/10.1186/s12978-020-00924-9

Fong, B. Y. F. (2019). Quality assurance procedures in private and public practice. *Medicine and Law, 38*(1), 127–142.

Foreign, Commonwealth & Development Office, Government of United Kingdom. (2021). *Ending preventable deaths of mothers, babies and children by 2030: Approach paper.* https://www.gov.uk/government/publications/ending-preventable-deaths-of-mothers-babies-and-children-by-2030/ending-preventable-deaths-of-mothers-babies-and-children-by-2030-approach-paper#executive-summary

Hoffman, S. J., Poirier, M. J. P., Rogers Van Katwyk, S., Baral, P., & Sritharan, L. (2019). Impact of the WHO framework convention on tobacco control on global cigarette consumption: Quasi-experimental evaluations using interrupted time series analysis and in-sample forecast event modelling. *BMJ, 365,* Article 12287. https://doi.org/10.1136/bmj.12287

Khetrapal, S., & Bhatia, R. (2020). Impact of COVID-19 pandemic on health system & Sustainable Development Goal 3. *The Indian Journal of Medical Research, 151*(5), 395–399. https://doi.org/10.4103/ijmr.IJMR_1920_20

32   *Ben Y. F. Fong*

Kruk, M. E., Gage, A. D., Arsenault, C., Jordan, K., Leslie, H. H., Roder-DeWan, S. et al. (2018). High-quality health systems in the sustainable development goals era: Time for a revolution. *The Lancet Global Health Commission, 6*(11), E1196–E1252. https://doi.org/10.1016/S2214-109X(18)30386-3

Kupka, R. (2021). *Why we need a science policy panel on chemicals, waste and pollution.* https://sdg.iisd.org/commentary/guest-articles/why-we-need-a-science-policy-panel-on-chemicals-waste-and-pollution/

NCD Alliance. (2017). *First WHO forum on alcohol, drugs & addictive behaviours provokes discussion, illuminates challenges & opportunities.* https://ncdalliance.org/news-events/blog/first-who-forum-on-alcohol-drugs-addictive-behaviours-provokes-discussion-illuminates-challenges-opportunities

National Road Safety Strategy. (n.d.). *Global road safety.* https://www.roadsafety.gov.au/global

Panichkriangkrai, W., Topothai, C., Saengruang, N., Thammatach-aree, J., & Tangcharoensathien, V. (2020). Universal access to sexual and reproductive health services in Thailand: Achievements and challenges. *Sexual and Reproductive Health Matters, 28*(2), Article 1805842. https://doi.org/10.1080/26410397.2020.1805842

United Nations Development Program. (2008). *MDG good practices–Scaling up efforts on the ground.* United Nations Development Group. https://www.undp.org/sites/g/files/zskgke326/files/publications/MDGGoodPractices.pdf

UN Environment. (2017). *Submission by UN environment to the office of the UN high commissioner on human rights: HRC resolution 35/23.* https://www.ohchr.org/sites/default/files/Documents/Issues/ESCR/SDG/UNEP.pdf

van Weel, C., & Kidd, M. R. (2018). Why strengthening primary health care is essential to achieving universal health coverage. *CMAJ, 190*(15), E463–E466. https://doi.org/10.1503/cmaj.170784

Varghese, C. (2017). Reducing premature mortality from non-communicable diseases, including for people with severe mental disorders. *World Psychiatry, 16*(1), 45–47. https://doi.org/10.1002/wps.20376

World Economic Forum. (2020). *Healthy futures: What are the challenges in making healthcare more sustainable?* https://www.weforum.org/agenda/2020/09/challenges-healthcare-sustainable-development-sdg3-good-health-well-being/

World Health Organization. (n.d.a). *Universal Health Coverage.* https://www.who.int/data/gho/data/themes/topics/sdg-target-3_3-communicable-diseases

World Health Organization. (n.d.b). *SDG target 3.3 communicable diseases.* https://www.who.int/health-topics/universal-health-coverage#tab=tab_1

World Health Organization. (2002). *Implications of the Doha Declaration on the TRIPS agreement and public health / Carlos M. Correa.* World Health Organization. https://apps.who.int/iris/handle/10665/67345

World Health Organization. (2007). *Everybody's business -- Strengthening health systems to improve health outcomes.* https://www.who.int/publications/i/item/everybody-s-business----strengthening-health-systems-to-improve-health-outcomes

World Health Organization. (2017). *Monitoring the health-related sustainable development goals (SDGs).* https://www.who.int/docs/default-source/searo/hsd/hwf/01-monitoring-the-health-related-sdgs-background-paper.pdf?sfvrsn=3417607a_4

World Health Organization. (2020). *Ending preventable newborn deaths and stillbirths by 2030: Moving faster towards high-quality universal health coverage in 2020–2025.* https://www.unicef.org/media/77166/file/Ending-preventable-newborn-deaths-and-stillbirths-by-2030-universal-health-coverage-in-2020%E2%80%932025.pdf

3 Sustainable Healthcare Financing for Universal Health Coverage

Tommy K. C. Ng and Ben Y. F. Fong

Introduction

Ageing population is an inevitable issue worldwide because of increase in life expectancy and decline in birth rate in many countries. Ageing population leads to not only a burden to the healthcare system but also economic and social consequences (Légaré, 2015; Yenilmez, 2015). To overcome the impact of ageing population, maintaining good health is the key to great opportunities for the society (Fried, 2016). Therefore, good population health is an attainable goal under ageing population. The purpose of achieving universal health coverage is to promote health for all by providing accessible, affordable and quality care to everyone without discrimination or preset conditions, meeting the health needs of the population. To facilitate the achievement of universal health coverage, the development of health infrastructure, particularly the primary healthcare service, is an important process (Kapologwe et al., 2020). Strong healthcare system with sustainable financing is also vital for moving towards universal health coverage. This means to treat healthcare as an economic good and therefore addressing market failures to ensure efficient and equitable health services (Kabaniha et al., 2021). Public financing is often not sufficient to raise the funding for health to achieve financial protection or expand health service coverage. Ensuring the mobility of funding and the efficient utilisation of funding are aligned with the objective of sustainable healthcare financing. Additionally, prioritising investments in primary healthcare is a crucial step to universal health coverage (World Health Organization, 2019). Primary care should be the first contact point for citizens to access health care service, and so good physical status and function of primary health service is vital for achieving universal health coverage.

Compared with other parts of the world, the Asia-Pacific region is facing a more rapid ageing situation. More than 10% of the population

DOI: 10.4324/9781003305637-3

in Eastern and South-Eastern Asia were aged 65 or above in 2019, and it was projected nearly one-fourth of the population in Eastern and South-Eastern Asia would be aged 65 or above in 2050 (United Nations, 2019). Besides, the proportion aged 65 or above in Australia and New Zealand is expected to increase from more than 15% in 2019 to more than 22% in 2050. Hong Kong, Japan, Singapore and Australia were ranked among the top ten life expectancy in the world (Worldometers, 2020). The highest current and future projections of ageing growth are in Eastern and South-Eastern Asia, Australia and New Zealand, reflecting ageing population is a big challenge in the Asia-Pacific region (Dhakal et al., 2022). In Japan, investments in primary, secondary and tertiary care were initiated in 1960, and the older people, despite high life expectancy, remain active and healthy (Barber & Rosenberg, 2017). It is worthwhile to understand how the Asia-Pacific region respond to the ageing population through health investments. In addition, moving towards universal health coverage is identified as a priority in many countries in order to ensure healthcare access to all citizens, and the population and direct health costs to be covered by pooled funds (Reich et al., 2016; Signorelli et al., 2020). Universal health coverage can bring better healthcare and service quality to the citizens. This chapter will compare different healthcare financing models in the Asia-Pacific region and identify how sustainable and equitable healthcare financing can be accomplished to ensure social and financial risk protection in terms of accessibility and universal health coverage leading to healthy lives and well-being for all at all ages.

Australia

The Australian Medicare was introduced by the Labour government in 1984 with the objective to promote equity by improving access and affordability of health services (Callander et al., 2019). Medicare allows the enrollees, including Australian and New Zealand citizens, to access public hospitals and academic medical centres, which are provided by independent medical practitioners, without financial barriers (Duckett, 2018). Two percent of the taxable income, known as the Medicare levy, is charged to citizens and Medicare enrollees for funding Medicare, except the low-income group (Services Australia, 2021). The Medicare Benefits Schedule lists out the medical service charges, set by the government, that the Australian government pays a Medicare rebate. Medicare can cover 100%, 85% and 75% of the Medicare Benefits Schedule fee for consultations provided by a general practitioner, all other services provided by a medical practitioner in the community and all private services, respectively (Caplan & Scott, 2022). Therefore, patients need to pay the doctors' charge when the charge is more than the Medicare rebate (Pulok et al., 2020). Some private medical services may need to be paid by patients' out-of-pocket unless the doctor bulk bills. The Medicare covers partly the healthcare charge in private healthcare.

A comprehensive primary care service is a key to improve health quality and equity. In 2015, the Australian government had launched Primary Health Networks to increase the efficacy and effectiveness of medical services and to improve the coordination of care (Department of Health, 2016). Primary Health Networks are independent companies working with existing services in both the public and private sectors (Booth & Boxall, 2016; Henderson et al., 2018). Needs assessment is undertaken to identify the at-risk and underserved population. Productive and collaborative partnership between local service providers and community is established under Primary Health Networks. The control of service specifications and reduction of conflict of interest could facilitate the equity in primary care in Australia, but the insufficient availability of services to rural communities could still hinder the equity in primary care (Henderson et al., 2018). The Primary Health Networks have fostered the development of good relationships between states primary healthcare actors and led to improvements in health care (Freeman et al., 2021).

Although universal health coverage has been established in Australia long time ago, the effectiveness and patient outcome of the healthcare system can still be improved. Since all Australian residents are enrolled in Medicare, they are entitled to access healthcare service with low cost or free of charge. However, there are shortcomings in the performance of the system. For example, the prevalence of obesity, one of the health risk factors, among Australian adults was 27.9% in 2015, and the average of the Organisation for Economic Co-operation and Development countries was 19.5% (Organisation for Economic Co-operation and Development, 2017). Besides, Dixit and Sambasivan (2018) had found that the waiting time from assessment to treatment by specialists for four surgery categories in Australia was longer than Canada, which has a healthcare system similar to Australia. It reflects that the efficiency in this area can be improved. For the out-of-pocket healthcare spending, the Australian patients spent more than the Canadians (Dixit & Sambasivan, 2018). In addition, inequalities of healthcare expenditure were found in Australia because low-income groups were more likely to spend 10% of more of household income on healthcare than high-income group (Callander et al., 2019). It was alarming to note that one-fourth of the Australian adults with chronic diseases would skip care because of the costs (Callander et al., 2017). These findings ascertain that although universal health coverage is provided, financial protection to ensure access to healthcare is essential, particularly for the low-income groups of citizens who are vulnerable in the community. So affordability of the healthcare service is one of the barriers to access healthcare among people.

Hong Kong

Hong Kong, one of the prosperous cities of China, has achieved the highest life expectancy in the world. With the growth of the population and the increase in healthcare needs, the total public health expenditure by the government was doubled from HK$90 billion in 2009/2010 to HK$189 billion in 2019/2020 (Food and Health Bureau, 2021). Population ageing is an important factor on the growth of healthcare expenditure (de Meijer et al., 2013). The healthcare system in Hong Kong is a dual-track system, supported by both public and private sectors. The share of public health expenditure was nearly half of the total health expenditure, while another half was spent on the private sector (Food and Health Bureau, 2021). The public health spending is funded under government schemes and mainly financed the inpatient service and ambulatory health service. The healthcare services in public sector are at low costs to the users, HK$50 and HK$75 for each general outpatient attendance and inpatient service admission, respectively, and HK$135 for the first attendance of specialist outpatient service. Therefore, Hong Kong residents can enjoy readily affordable healthcare services in the public sector. People who have financial difficulties, such as recipients of Comprehensive Social Security Assistance, can apply for medical fee waiver. Hence, all Hong Kong citizens can enjoy affordable healthcare services. Nevertheless, the waiting time for public health services, especially accident and emergency services, specialist outpatient clinics and ambulatory diagnostic services are long, due to over-reliance of these services by the community and the shortage of manpower in the Hospital Authority that manages all public hospitals and specialist clinics. For outpatient services, the longest waiting time for ophthalmology, surgery and traumatology were 164 weeks, 104 weeks and 116 weeks, respectively, between April 2021 and March 2022 (Hospital Authority, 2022). Besides, the waiting time of some of the urgent, semi-urgent and stable cases of ambulatory diagnostic services were increased from 2016–2017 to 2018–2019 (The

Government of the Hong Kong Special Administrative Region, 2019). To encourage appropriate use of public health services, the charges at public hospitals were increased, ranging from 9% to 80%, in 2017 (The Government of the Hong Kong Special Administrative Region, 2017), but there is no improvement in the waiting time for the services.

The Hong Kong government wanted to reduce the over-reliance of public health service by shifting to using more private sector and at the same time, to achieve universal health coverage. It had implemented several health policies, such as Elderly Health Care Voucher Scheme (EHCVS) (Department of Health, 2020) and Voluntary Health Insurance Scheme (VHIS) (Food and Health Bureau, 2019). EHCVS, which aims to enhance the use of private primary care and reduce the financial burden on medical services among residents aged 65 or above, has been modified since its inception in 2014, and currently the accumulated limit of unused vouchers was increased to HK$8,000 in 2019 (Department of Health, 2020). However, the effectiveness of this scheme is considered to be doubtful. Both healthcare professionals and older adults revealed that the low pricing of services in the public sector and expensive private healthcare were the main barriers to shifting users from the public to the private sector (Fung et al., 2022; Lai et al., 2018). The impact of the voucher scheme on changing the pattern of service utilisation by older adults was found to be insignificant, and EHCVS was unable to relieve the burden of over-utilisation of public healthcare services even after the voucher amounts had been increased substantially (Chong et al., 2021). Therefore, the voucher scheme has not achieved the original purpose of its establishment.

Apart from EHCVS, the Hong Kong government introduced the VHIS in 2019 (Food and Health Bureau, 2019). This scheme is a voluntary and government-regulated private medical insurance programme which provides the public an additional choice of insurance for using private healthcare services (Yin & He, 2018). Tax deduction is an incentive to encourage people to take up the VHIS. Before its implementation, a research found that one-third of the respondents had intention to subscribe to the scheme but people without any insurance did not show interest to participate in this scheme (He, 2017). Two years after the implementation of the scheme, the number of participants was only 791,000, which is 10.7% of the total population in Hong Kong (Legislative Council, 2021). Since the cost and quality of public healthcare service can provide a safety net for all residents, the older groups and higher health risks groups will be least attracted to the VHIS (Chan, 2021).

Universal health coverage is achievable in Hong Kong with the current healthcare financing policy because public healthcare services are provided at low or even no cost for all eligible residents and people in need. All citizens can enjoy accessible and affordable healthcare services. Nevertheless, the low cost services are leading to over-reliance of the heavily subsidised public healthcare services and, as a consequence of the great demand, long waiting time of the services, particularly specialist consultations. The EHCVS and VHIS launched in recent years have not helped to relieve the burden in the public sector, and their overall effectiveness remains unsatisfactory. Likewise, quality of services in the public sector is negatively affected, and there is room for improvement (Wong et al., 2010).

India

India has a population accounting for more than 17% of the total population in the world in 2019 and it is expected to increase with more than 270 million people between 2019 and 2050 (United Nations, 2019). Private healthcare is dominant in India and catered for three-fourth of the out-patients and more than 60% of the in-patients services (Rout et al., 2019). India cannot meet the average of the universal health coverage among the world (World Health Organization, 2019). Their progress in this aspect falls behind among the Asia-Pacific regions, despite the discussion on universal health coverage made in 1946 (Devadasan et al., 2014). In 2017, India had stated to prioritise the achievement of universal health coverage in the National Health Policy 2017 (Ministry of Health and Family Welfare, 2017). The Ayushman Bharat Programme, which aimed to provide universal health coverage to the population, was announced and approved by the Indian government to provide financial health protection to the vulnerable and needy citizens (Angell et al., 2019; Lahariya, 2018). The programme has two components, including (1) upgrading most of the Health and Wellness Centres to provide primary care services and free essential drugs, and (2) providing a coverage of around US$7,700 per family per year (covering about 500 million of Indian who are below the poverty line) for secondary and tertiary medical expenses (Joseph et al., 2021; Lahariya, 2018). The programme aims to increase the accessibility, affordability and quality of healthcare service.

The household out-of-pocket expenditure on health was decreased from 69.4% in 2004–2005 to 48.8% in 2017–2018 (Ministry of Health & Family Welfare, 2021). This reflected that the Indian government had put more resources on healthcare after prioritising the universal health coverage. Similarly, primary healthcare services in India were strengthened after the implementation of the Ayushman Bharat Programme with provision of free medicines, establishment of Health Management Information System and strengthening the participation of community in health services (Lahariya, 2020). However, there is inequality in healthcare utilisation among older adults because the elderly living in urban India are using more healthcare services than those in rural areas (Banerjee, 2021). It is found that the level of education and economic status are the determinants of such difference, but this situation can be improved through related policies by the government for better quality of life for the population and universal health coverage.

Japan

Japan, one of the countries with the longest life expectancy in the world, had faced the issues of population ageing long time ago. The Japanese healthcare system has been rated satisfactory in terms of availability, effectiveness and quality at reasonably low cost (Hiromasa, 2022; Zhang & Oyama, 2016). Social health insurance was extended to the entire population in Japan in 1961 so that universal health coverage was achieved (Ikegami et al., 2011). All employees have to be enrolled in the employee-based plans and the self-employed, unemployed and retirees under 75 years have to enroll in residence-based national health insurance. Citizens who are aged 75 and above needs to enroll in Health Insurance for the Elderly (Japan Health Policy NOW, 2018). Citizens have to co-pay for the medical costs but the co-payments vary for different groups. The percentages of co-payments are 30% for residents aged 69 or below, 20% for those aged under 6 and between 70 and 74, and 10% for low-income earners aged 75 and over. Private health sector is predominant in Japan, where clinics and hospitals found by national and local governments were accounted for 3.8% and 15.0%, respectively, in 2014 (Matsuda, 2016).

   The social health insurance seems to cover all citizens in Japan for them to enjoy accessible and affordable healthcare services but there are some challenges in this healthcare financing arrangement. The unemployed residents can enroll in the residence-based national health insurance but their health coverage can be lost if they fail to pay premiums for more than one year (Matsuda, 2016). Some residents had to delay medical consultations or even stop their treatment due to the loss of job, which results in the loss of their employee-based insurance plan (Matsuda, 2016; Japan Federation of Democratic Medical Institutions, 2021). Without health insurance, citizens have to pay high amount of out-of-pocket money for the treatment and consultations. Those who are unemployed and aged under 70 may not able to have access to healthcare services timely. The universal health coverage is positively associated with the health-related quality of life but the vulnerable group, particularly the low incomers, needs to be protected under the well-established health financing system. In response to the economic recession under COVID-19 pandemic, the Japanese government had implemented Special Cash Payment programme, which provided a one-off payment of US$1,000 to each resident, to relieve financial difficulties in this situation. The Special Cash Payment programme was found to have positive impact on the individuals' health-related quality of life (Ikeda et al., 2022). Hence, people could use the financial support to sustain their health insurance even when there was loss of income and unemployment.

In view of the ageing society and the needs of the long-term care, the Japan government has implemented long-term care insurance, which is financed through premium contributions and general taxation (Luk, 2020). People who are (1) aged 65 or above or (2) with disability and aged between 40 and 64 can enroll in this programme and receive the long-term care service. With the ageing society, implementation of long-term care insurance also leads to some critical concerns, such as fiscal sustainability and shortage of healthcare professionals (Luk, 2020). The cost for long-term care service was dramatically increased due to increase in the number of eligible people and demand for long-term care service. Hence, the premiums and user co-payments were increased to sustain the system, adding financial burden to the enrollees. Furthermore, the working population is shrinking due to the ageing population, causing shortage of healthcare professionals.

The universal health coverage in Japan is well-established for a long time and guarantees the accessibility of healthcare services for the entire population. Nevertheless, some vulnerable groups, such as low income, may not be able to sustain their social health insurance to continue their medical treatment. Besides, the ageing population leads to heavy financial burden to citizens and government. Therefore, a new approach of funding by considering private health insurance may improve the sustainability of the health financing for universal health coverage in Japan (Kosaka & Kondo, 2020).

Conclusion

The life expectancy of population is increasing but the fertility rate is decreasing in many countries, particularly in the Asia-Pacific region, where most countries are facing the new challenges arising from ageing population. The United Nations had suggested various sustainable development goals, including achieve universal health coverage, by 2030 to address global challenges. In the sustainable development goal 3, universal health coverage is one of the targets to be achieved and it leads many countries, especially the developing countries, to review and revise their healthcare financing models. Achieving universal health coverage is beneficial to the health of the population and sustainable development of the country, and governments should examine new ways to invest more on healthcare financing. Different healthcare financing strategies are adopted in different countries and cities. There is no absolutely perfect financing scheme because of many determinants, such as demographic and socio-economic status of the population. National research on healthcare financing is important to understand and ascertain the effectiveness of health coverage and sustainability of financing the services, particularly when dealing with an increasing ageing population.

References

Angell, B. J., Prinja, S., Gupt, A., Jha, V., & Jan, S. (2019). The Ayushman Bharat Pradhan Mantri Jan Arogya Yojana and the path to universal health coverage in India: Overcoming the challenges of stewardship and governance. *PLoS Medicine, 16*(3), Article e1002759. https://doi.org/10.1371/journal.pmed.1002759

Banerjee, S. (2021). Determinants of rural-urban differential in healthcare utilization among the elderly population in India. *BMC Public Health, 21*, Article 939. https://doi.org/10.1186/s12889-021-10773-1

Barber, S. L., & Rosenberg, M. (2017). Aging and universal health coverage: Implications for the Asia Pacific region. *Health Systems & Reform, 3*(3), 154–158. https://doi.org/10.1080/23288604.2017.1348320

Booth, M., & Boxall, A. M. (2016). Commissioning services and primary health networks. *Australian Journal of Primary Health, 22*(1), 3–4. https://doi.org/10.1071/PY15167

Callander, E. J., Corscadden, L., & Levesque, J. F. (2017). Out-of-pocket healthcare expenditure and chronic disease–do Australians forgo care because of the cost? *Australian Journal of Primary Health, 23*(1), 15–22. https://doi.org/10.1071/PY16005

Callander, E. J., Fox, H., & Lindsay, D. (2019). Out-of-pocket healthcare expenditure in Australia: Trends, inequalities and the impact on household living standards in a high-income country with a universal health care system. *Health Economics Review, 9,* Article 10. https://doi.org/10.1186/s13561-019-0227-9

Caplan, G. A., & Scott, T. A. (2022). Systems of healthcare: Australia. In A. J. Sinclair, J. E. Morley, B. Vellas, M. Cesari, & M. Munshi (Eds.), *Pathy's Principles and Practice of Geriatric Medicine* (pp. 1603–1608). John Wiley & Sons Ltd. https://doi.org/10.1002/9781119484288.ch129

Chan, R. K. (2021). Politics matters: The attempts and failure of health finance reform in Hong Kong. In Information Resources Management Association (Ed.), *Research Anthology on Public Health Services, Policies, and Education* (pp. 565–575). IGI Global. https://doi.org/10.4018/978-1-7998-8960-1.ch025

Chong, K. C., Fung, H., Yam, C. H. K., Chau, P. Y. K., Chow, T. Y., Zee, B. C. Y.,... & Yeoh, E. K. (2021). Long-term effectiveness of elderly health care voucher scheme strategies: A system dynamics simulation analysis. *BMC Public Health, 21,* Article 1235. https://doi.org/10.1186/s12889-021-11280-z

de Meijer, C., Wouterse, B., Polder, J., & Koopmanschap, M. (2013). The effect of population aging on health expenditure growth: A critical review. *European Journal of Ageing, 10*(4), 353–361. https://doi.org/10.1007/s10433-013-0280-x

Department of Health. (2016). *Primary health networks grant programme guidelines.* https://www.health.gov.au/sites/default/files/documents/2021/04/primary-health-networks-phn-grant-program-guidelines-phn-grant-program-guidelines.pdf

Department of Health. (2020). *Health care voucher.* https://www.hcv.gov.hk/eng/index.htm

Dhakal, S. P., Burgess, J., & Nankervis, A. (2022). Population ageing: Challenges in the Asia Pacific and Beyond. In S. Dhakal, A. Nankervis & J. Burgess (Eds.), *Ageing Asia and the Pacific in Changing Times* (pp. 3–15). Springer. https://doi.org/10.1007/978-981-16-6663-6_1

Dixit, S. K., & Sambasivan, M. (2018). A review of the Australian healthcare system: A policy perspective. *SAGE Open Medicine, 6,* 1–14. https://doi.org/10.1177/2050312118769211

Duckett, S. (2018). Expanding the breadth of Medicare: Learning from Australia. *Health Economics, Policy and Law, 13*(3–4), 344–368. https://doi.org/10.1017/S1744133117000421

Food and Health Bureau. (2019). *About VHIS.* https://www.vhis.gov.hk/en/about_us/index.html

Food and Health Bureau. (2021). *Hong Kong's domestic health accounts (DHA).* https://www.fhb.gov.hk/statistics/download/dha/en/a_estimate_1920.pdf

Freeman, T., Baum, F., Javanparast, S., Ziersch, A., Mackean, T., & Windle, A. (2021). Challenges facing primary health care in federated government systems: Implementation of Primary Health Networks in Australian states and territories. *Health Policy, 125*(4), 495–503. https://doi.org/10.1016/j.healthpol.2021.02.002

Fried, L. P. (2016). Investing in health to create a third demographic dividend. *The Gerontologist, 56*(Suppl_2), S167-S177. https://doi.org/10.1093/geront/gnw035

Fung, V. L. H., Lai, A. H. Y., Yam, C. H. K., Wong, E. L. Y., Griffiths, S. M., & Yeoh, E. K. (2022). Healthcare vouchers for better elderly services? Input from private healthcare service providers in Hong Kong. *Health & Social Care in the Community, 30*(2), e357–e369. https://doi.org/10.1111/hsc.13203

He, A. J. (2017). Introducing voluntary private health insurance in a mixed medical economy: Are Hong Kong citizens willing to subscribe? *BMC Health Services Research, 17*, Article 603. https://doi.org/10.1186/s12913-017-2559-7

Henderson, J., Javanparast, S., MacKean, T., Freeman, T., Baum, F., & Ziersch, A. (2018). Commissioning and equity in primary care in Australia: Views from primary health networks. *Health & Social Care in the Community, 26*(1), 80–89. https://doi.org/10.1111/hsc.12464

Hiromasa, S. (2022). Healthcare system and hospital management in Japan: Focusing on the management accounting system from the perspective of quality of care. In T. Matsuo & Y. Shima (Eds.), *Management Accounting For Healthcare* (pp. 51–74). World Scientific. https://doi.org/10.1142/9789811237164_0003

Hospital Authority. (2022). *Waiting Time for Stable New Case Booking at Specialist Out-patient Clinics.* https://www.ha.org.hk/haho/ho/sopc/dw_wait_ls_eng.pdf

Ikeda, T., Igarashi, A., Odani, S., Murakami, M., & Tabuchi, T. (2022). Health-related quality of life during COVID-19 pandemic: Assessing impacts of job loss and financial support programs in Japan. *Applied Research in Quality of Life, 17*(2), 541–557. https://doi.org/10.1007/s11482-021-09918-6

Ikegami, N., Yoo, B. K., Hashimoto, H., Matsumoto, M., Ogata, H., Babazono, A.,... & Kobayashi, Y. (2011). Japanese universal health coverage: Evolution, achievements, and challenges. *The Lancet, 378*(9796), 1106–1115. https://doi.org/10.1016/S0140-6736(11)60828-3

Japan Federation of Democratic Medical Institutions. (2021). *2020 late death case survey summary table due to financial reasons (uninsured, qualification, short-term certificate (in Japanese).* https://www.min-iren.gr.jp/wp-content/uploads/2021/03/210621_02.pdf

Japan Health Policy NOW. (2018). *Japan's Health Insurance System.* http://japanhpn.org/en/section-3-1/

Joseph, J., Sankar D, H., & Nambiar, D. (2021). Empanelment of health care facilities under Ayushman Bharat Pradhan Mantri Jan Arogya Yojana (AB PM-JAY) in India. *PLoS One, 16*(5), Article e0251814. https://doi.org/10.1371/journal.pone.0251814

Kabaniha, G.A., Ataguba, J.EO., Kutzin, J. (2021). Global health-care financing. In R. Haring, I. Kickbusch, D. Ganten, & M. Moeti (Eds.), *Handbook of Global Health.* Springer, Cham. https://doi.org/10.1007/978-3-030-05325-3_68-2

Kapologwe, N. A., Meara, J. G., Kengia, J. T., Sonda, Y., Gwajima, D., Alidina, S., & Kalolo, A. (2020). Development and upgrading of public primary healthcare facilities with essential surgical services infrastructure: A strategy towards achieving universal health coverage in Tanzania. *BMC Health Services Research, 20,* Article 218. https://doi.org/10.1186/s12913-020-5057-2

Kosaka, M., & Kondo, M. (2020). Universal health coverage and private health insurance in Japan: From policy research to practice. In T. Hasegawa, T. Hasegawa, T. Hirao, M. Kondo & S. Mehra (Eds.), *Health care policy in East Asia: A world scientific reference: Volume 2: Health care system reform and policy research in Japan* (pp. 265–274). World Scientific Series in Global Health Economics and Public Policy. https://doi.org/10.1142/9789813236141_0019

Lahariya, C. (2018). 'Ayushman Bharat'program and universal health coverage in India. *Indian Pediatrics, 55*(6), 495–506. https://doi.org/10.1007/s13312-018-1341-1

Lahariya, C. (2020). Health & wellness centers to strengthen primary health care in India: Concept, progress and ways forward. *The Indian Journal of Pediatrics, 87*(11), 916–929. https://doi.org/10.1007/s12098-020-03359-z

Lai, A. H. Y., Kuang, Z., Yam, C. H. K., Ayub, S., & Yeoh, E. K. (2018). Vouchers for primary healthcare services in an ageing world? The perspectives of elderly voucher recipients in Hong Kong. *Health & Social Care in the Community, 26*(3), 374–382. https://doi.org/10.1111/hsc.12523

Légaré, J. (2015). Population aging: Economic and social consequences. *International Encyclopedia of the Social & Behavioral Sciences (Second Edition), 2015,* 540–544. https://doi.org/10.1016/B978-0-08-097086-8.34041-7

Legislative Council. (2021). *Update on the voluntary health insurance scheme.* https://www.legco.gov.hk/yr20-21/english/panels/hs/papers/hs20210709cb4-1196-5-e.pdf

Luk, S. C. Y. (2020). Japan: The long-term care insurance reform. In S. C. Y. Luk (Ed.), *Ageing, long-term care insurance and healthcare finance in Asia* (pp. 60–78). Routledge. https://doi.org/10.4324/9781315115689-4

Matsuda, R. (2016). Public/private health care delivery in Japan: And some gaps in "universal" coverage. *Global Social Welfare, 3*(3), 201–212. https://doi.org/10.1007/s40609-016-0073-1

Ministry of Health and Family Welfare. (2017). *National health policy 2017.* https://www.nhp.gov.in//NHPfiles/national_health_policy_2017.pdf

Ministry of Health & Family Welfare. (2021). *National health accounts estimates for India 2017–18.* https://nhsrcindia.org/sites/default/files/2021-11/National%20Health%20Accounts-%202017-18.pdf

Organisation for Economic Co-operation and Development. (2017). *Obesity update 2017.* https://www.oecd.org/health/health-systems/Obesity-Update-2017.pdf

Pulok, M. H., van Gool, K., & Hall, J. (2020). Horizontal inequity in the utilisation of healthcare services in Australia. *Health Policy, 124*(11), 1263–1271. https://doi.org/10.1016/j.healthpol.2020.08.012

Reich, M. R., Harris, J., Ikegami, N., Maeda, A., Cashin, C., Araujo, E. C.,... & Evans, T. G. (2016). Moving towards universal health coverage: Lessons from 11 country studies. *The Lancet, 387*(10020), 811–816. https://doi.org/10.1016/S0140-6736(15)60002-2

Rout, S. K., Sahu, K. S., & Mahapatra, S. (2021). Utilization of health care services in public and private healthcare in India: Causes and determinants. *International Journal of Healthcare Management, 14*(2), 509–516. https://doi.org/10.1080/20479700.2019.1665882

Services Australia. (2021). *Medicare and tax.* https://www.servicesaustralia.gov.au/medicare-and-tax?context=60092#medicarelevy

Signorelli, C., Odone, A., Oradini-Alacreu, A., & Pelissero, G. (2020). Universal Health Coverage in Italy: Lights and shades of the Italian National Health Service which celebrated its 40th anniversary. *Health Policy, 124*(1), 69–74. https://doi.org/10.1016/j.healthpol.2019.11.002

The Government of the Hong Kong Special Administrative Region. (2017). *Fees and charges at public hospitals to be revised next month.* https://www.info.gov.hk/gia/general/201705/22/P2017052200538.htm?fontSize=1

The Government of the Hong Kong Special Administrative Region. (2019). *LCQ20: Waiting Time for the Services of Specialist Outpatient Clinics and Ambulatory Diagnostic Services in Public Hospitals.* https://www.info.gov.hk/gia/general/201904/17/P2019041700580.htm

United Nations. (2019). *World population prospects 2019 highlights.* https://population.un.org/wpp/Publications/Files/WPP2019_Highlights.pdf

Wong, S., Kung, K., Griffiths, S. M., Carthy, T., Wong, M., Lo, S. V.,... & Starfield, B. (2010). Comparison of primary care experiences among adults in general outpatient clinics and private general practice clinics in Hong Kong. *BMC Public Health, 10*, Article 397. https://doi.org/10.1186/1471-2458-10-397

Worldometers. (2020). *Life expectancy of the world population.* https://www.worldometers.info/demographics/life-expectancy/

World Health Organization. (2019). *Primary health care on the road to universal health coverage 2019 monitoring report.* https://www.who.int/docs/default-source/documents/2019-uhc-report.pdf

Yenilmez, M. I. (2015). Economic and social consequences of population aging the dilemmas and opportunities in the twenty-first century. *Applied Research in Quality of Life, 10*(4), 735–752. https://doi.org/10.1007/s11482-014-9334-2

Yin, J. D. C., & He, A. J. (2018). Health insurance reforms in Singapore and Hong Kong: How the two ageing Asian tigers respond to health financing challenges? *Health Policy, 122*(7), 693–697. https://doi.org/10.1016/j.healthpol.2018.04.012

Zhang, X., & Oyama, T. (2016). Investigating the health care delivery system in Japan and reviewing the local public hospital reform. *Risk Management and Healthcare Policy, 9*, 21–32. https://doi.org/10.2147/RMHP.S93285

4 Development of Healthcare Professionals and Leadership in Achieving Sustainability

Kar-wai Tong

Introduction

Health has become a universally recognised human right since the establishments of the United Nations (UN) and the World Health Organization (WHO) (Zakus & Cortinois 2002, pp. 40–41). The Constitution of the WHO (1946, Preamble) has embedded "the highest attainable standard of health" as one of the principles "basic to the happiness, harmonious relations and security of all peoples". Their freedoms from interference and entitlements to equal access to health services without discrimination serve as two fundamental guidelines to materialise this basic human right (United Nations Committee on Economic, Social and Cultural Rights of the Economic and Social Council, 2000). In practice, the degree of protecting health as a basic right is subject to a number of considerations at the national and domestic levels, for example, social determinants of health (World Health Organization, 2022b), people's socio-economic statuses (World Health Organization, 2018), healthcare expenditures and people's ability to make co-payments (World Health Organization, 2019), and how a country sees the right to health as a constitutional right and/or a statutory right and whether appropriate practical measures are in place to ensure the protection of this right (Kinney & Clark, 2004; Tobin, 2012).

Global Shortage of Healthcare Workforce

A WHO report with a title of *"A universal truth: No health without a workforce"* has highlighted in a loud and clear tone the importance of healthcare workforce (Campbell et al., 2013). In addition to social, financial and legal concerns, the long-term global shortage of healthcare workforce is another significant factor threatening the protection of health as a basic right, the quality of healthcare services and the

DOI: 10.4324/9781003305637-4

sustainability of healthcare systems; and the shortage was estimated at 17.4 million in 2013, and it would still stand high at 14 million in 2030 worldwide, with Southeast Asia and Africa facing the most serious challenges (World Health Organization, 2016). More than just numerical figures, the "double whammy" of an ageing population, in general, and an ageing healthcare workforce, in particular, has intensified the urgency for governments to deal with the shortage (Buchan & Campbell, 2013). Low fertility rate may also have a bearing on the supply of healthcare personnel (Wu et al., 2021). Other circumstances such as the tremendous pressure exerted by the outbreak of COVID-19 (World Health Organization, 2022d) leading to elective surgery backlog (Magennis et al., 2022), for example, have further exacerbated the issues of healthcare workforce shortage.

On top of the macro-level considerations like population ageing, low fertility rate and epidemiological impact, human resources management concerns arising from financial and non-financial incentives for healthcare professionals (Lee et al., 2019), appropriate staff mix with necessary skills and training (McPake et al., 2013), staff absenteeism (Ramadhan & Santoso, 2015), inequitable availability of healthcare professionals in rural and remote districts, high staff turnover rates and ineffective policy management (Portela et al., 2017), etc., are also common internationally. The WHO (2006) has devised a theoretical framework (Figure 4.1) to address the needs of healthcare workforce at different stages, from their entry, through to serving as a member of the workforce, and eventually to their exit. In this theoretical framework, governments are advised to (a) better prepare the healthcare workforce through appropriate policy planning, education and recruitment, (b) enhance their performance and productivity in service through proper supervision, reliable compensation, system supports, and continuous professional development, and (c) deal with "manpower wastage" issues like migration, occupational safety and health and retirement. In practice, it is easier said than done and governments face different challenges.

Healthcare financing is one of the government headaches, as healthcare workforce is labour intensive and costly (Buchan & Poz, 2003; Lee et al., 2019). Developed countries have spent a substantial percentage of GDP for healthcare services, amounting to, for instance, 17.0% in the United States, 12.1% in Switzerland, 11.7% in Germany, 10.3% in the United Kingdom, and 9.3% in Australia in 2019 (Health Bureau of Hong Kong, 2022c, Table 5.1). If "[h]ealth is … seen as a resource for everyday life … emphasising social and personal resources, as well as physical capacities" as stated in the Ottawa Charter for Health Promotion 1986

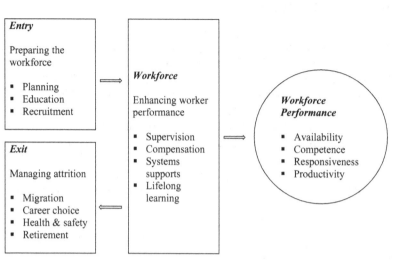

Figure 4.1 Working Lifespan Strategies (adapted from World Health Organization, 2006, p. xxi, Figure 4).

(World Health Organization, 1986, the first paragraph), a competent healthcare workforce is one of the essential "raw" resources to underpin health as a daily resource for individuals. Countries have to pay a high price for such "raw" resources, as staff cost generally constitutes a significant ratio of the total healthcare expenditures. In Tajikistan, the cost of healthcare staff in the public sector was reported alarmingly to be more than 90% of its budget (World Health Organization Regional Office for Europe, 2021). In Hong Kong, staff cost in public hospitals accounts for around 70% of the annual total operating expenses, which has already been reduced from the past ratio of approximately 80% (Liu & Yue, 1998), and it was reported to be HK$57.7 billion out of the total expenditure at HK$84.7 billion in 2020–2021 (Hospital Authority of Hong Kong, 2021). In the United States, the cost of healthcare workforce was over 50% of the total expenditure of hospitals before the pandemic of COVID-19 and the financial commitments to staff costs during the pandemic have been even higher (American Hospital Association, 2022, p. 2). In the United Kingdom, the number of full-time equivalent employees of the National Health Service (NHS) in England was 1.2 million as of June 2021 and the staff cost was £56.1 billion in 2019–2020, representing 46.6% of its annual budget (The King's Fund, 2022). In Europe, the largest item in healthcare expenses is also staff cost (Thomson et al., 2014).

International Cooperation

The success in maintaining a stable global healthcare workforce requires international cooperation, on top of national policies and local strategies. To call for collaboration worldwide to address global healthcare challenges is not new, and health as a subject of international cooperation may be dated back to 1851 when the first International Sanitary Conference was held in Paris (Howard-Jones, 1975). Succeeding the Millennium Development Goals of the period 2000–2015 (World Health Organization, 2016), the UN adopted the 2030 Agenda for Sustainable Development Goals (SDGs) in 2015 (United Nations Development Programme, 2022). The 2030 Agenda appeals for member states' global partnership to take actions and measures to terminate poverty, conserve the Earth, and secure peace and prosperity for people, etc., by 2030, where there are a total of 17 SDGs, and, in particular, its Goal 3 concerns good health and well-being with 13 targets, specifying, among others, (a) the need for universal health coverage to allow people's access to quality essential healthcare services, medicine and vaccines in an affordable manner, and (b) the needs to increase healthcare financing significantly and to ensure the sustainable supply of healthcare workforce especially in least developed and small-island developing countries (United Nations Development Programme, 2022). To attain the goal of universal coverage, the World Health Assembly (WHA) resolved in the 58th meeting (World Health Organization, 2005) to encourage member states to share experiences on various health financing policies and schemes, including social health insurance programmes, to address and sustain healthcare financing.

As for the workforce concerns, shortly afterwards the adoption of the 2030 Agenda, the WHO (2016) published a document entitled *Global Strategy on Human Resources for Health: Workforce 2030*, listing possible policy options of general relevance for the consideration of member states. In fact, before the adoption of the Agenda 2030, the Global Health Workforce Alliance was formed in 2006, and it has been transformed into the Global Health Workforce Network since 2016 in support of the pursuit of the above *Global Strategy* (World Health Organization, 2022c). The 63th meeting of the WHA (World Health Organization, 2010), with deep concerns on the severe global shortage of healthcare workforce as a major threat to healthcare systems, also adopted in 2010 the "WHO Global Code of Practice on the International Recruitment of Health Personnel" (the WHO Code), aiming at, inter alia, encouraging ethical international recruitment of healthcare professionals (Article 1(1)) and strengthening member states' cooperation in such recruitment (Article 1(4)). The WHA followed up the implementation of the WHO Code in subsequent meetings; for instance, the WHA at the 64th meeting urged member states to implement the WHO Code on a voluntary basis, such that both source and destination countries, especially those facing severe healthcare workforce shortages, may benefit from the international migration of healthcare professionals and mitigate any possible negative impact on health systems arising from the migration (World Health Organization, 2011).

International cooperation as a solution to universal crises, however, "might not always be easy", as exemplified by what Tedros Adhanom Ghebreyesus, WHO Director-General, said in 2020 in a conference on the pandemic of COVID-19 (Adhanom Ghebreyesus, 2020). With regard to international recruitment of healthcare professionals, the effectiveness of the WHO Code was doubted, as its implementation on a voluntary basis is a significant weakness (Aluttis et al., 2014). Three years after the adoption of the WHO Code (World Health Organization, 2010), the data in 2013 still showed a substantial increasing trend in the number of sub-Saharan African doctors working in the United States (Tankwanchi et al., 2014, p. e390). In the period of June 2019 to January 2020, an expert advisory group conducted a review of the WHO Code and confirmed its high relevance, but they also identified significant gaps in relation to its implementation, such as the lack of an updated list of countries with serious health workforce shortages as well as member states' ad hoc incorporation of the WHO Code into national law and policies, depending only on government leadership rather than targeted financial resources, which failed to benefit jurisdictions facing severely shortages of healthcare workforce and may become a tumbling block for the achievements of universal health coverage and SDGs (World Health Organization, 2020). In response to the report of this expert advisory group, the WHO (2021) prepared the Health Workforce Support and Safeguards List in 2021, containing a total of 47 countries with compelling health workforce needs.

Turning to the 2030 Agenda for Sustainable Development Goals, cooperation within a country has also been a concern. Member states of the WHO Regional Committee for Europe at the 67th session in 2017 endorsed a regional roadmap for the achievement of the 2030 Agenda, with the first survey in an electronic format being conducted in the period of July 2019 to February 2020 to examine member states' implementation of the roadmap (World Health Organization Regional Office for Europe, 2021). Among the 19 responding member states, "insufficient budget to meet the priorities" (68%) was considered to be the top barrier for the implementation of national health planning frameworks, followed by "low level of intersectoral cooperation and interaction" (32%), "ineffective mechanisms ensuring coordination and cooperation" and "limited partnership opportunities" (26% both), as well as "frequent changes of key staff" and "poor quality of statistical information" (21% both). In particular, Tajikistan elaborated that the high staff cost in the public healthcare sector, the staff shortage because of migration abroad and frequent changes in local management were hurdles for the execution of health and well-being priorities.

Government Strategies

Healthcare reform is a common government strategy to face the challenges in healthcare financing. In addition to increasing the number of places of students in traditional healthcare education and training programmes, reforms may comprise, for instance, reducing staff numbers and remunerations, changing skill mix, using telehealth and healthcare technologies to address staff shortages, as well as restructuring hospital services and cutting hospital budgets for cost savings (Thomson et al., 2014). Other measures may also consist of enhancing primary care, promoting public-private partnership, increasing tax and users' co-payments, and encouraging the use of personal health insurance, etc. (Food and Health Bureau of Hong Kong, 2008). With particular reference to healthcare workforce shortages, a few strategies are discussed below.

Use of Telehealth and Health Technologies

Telehealth and health technologies may help the delivery of healthcare in a more equitable and cost-savings manner (Wade et al., 2010), but they may not help fix the shortage of healthcare workforce. Telehealth systems enabling functions such as remote monitoring and online consultations may facilitate healthcare for patients at a remote area or at home, thus saving healthcare professionals' travelling time to see patients (Loh et al., 2013). Healthcare technological advancements like coronary angioplasty, which restores blood flow to the heart without traditional open-heart surgery, may help shorten patients' length of hospital stay (Astin, 2018), allowing the same healthcare workforce to serve more patients. The blooming artificial intelligence may even possibly "replace doctors with minimum errors" (Chikhaoui et al., 2022), and healthcare professionals who do not dance with artificial intelligence may "lose their jobs over time" (Davenport & Kalakota, 2019). That said, from the perspective of holistic care, it is not until a day when healthcare technologies have been "re-humanised" from "'high tech, no touch" medicine to "high-tech, hi-touch" medicine' (Shelley, 2016) that healthcare technological advancements could meet patient needs fully for human touch and care. For instance, in a study during the outbreak of COVID-19 to see if social robots could replace occupational therapists, the researchers found that while social robots may serve as a good companion for older persons, the conventional real-person group therapy mode had higher therapeutic factor scores than those through the robots (Liao et al., 2021). In another survey, the use of a chemotherapy-dispensing robot in a 2,500-bed health facility did not succeed in reducing the number of oncology pharmacists and technicians (Chen et al., 2013).

Recruiting Foreign-Trained Healthcare Professionals

To recruit foreign-trained healthcare professionals to address local shortages has been a common strategy worldwide (Bludau, 2021), but it is not a panacea. At the international level, the flow of healthcare professionals around the world has aroused debates on the global resultant impact on various healthcare systems, in terms of sustainability, justice and social accountabilities, as such migration, especially the outflow of healthcare workforce from developing to developed countries, has further caused the source countries to suffer from a continual brain drain (Aluttis et al., 2014). There has been an appeal for giving a stop to the "abusive" recruitments of doctors from developing countries (Feld, 2021).

At the professional level, how well would local professional bodies welcome migrant healthcare professionals? In Hong Kong, for example, the Medical Council of Hong Kong accepted medical qualifications of recognised Commonwealth countries before September 1996 and allowed overseas doctors to practise medicine in Hong Kong (Health Bureau of Hong Kong, 2022b), but after that date, the Medical Council tightened the admission policy and required non-locally trained doctors to take a three-part licensing examination with a one-year internship in approved public hospitals before they could apply for full-registration as a registered medical practitioner (Research Office of the Legislative Council Secretariat of Hong Kong, 2019). It was not until the passage of the contentious Medical Registration (Amendment) Bill 2021 in the legislature on 21 October 2021 that the long-haul debates were ended and some requirements were relaxed for non-locally trained medical graduates to practise medicine in Hong Kong (The Government of the Hong Kong Special Administrative Region, 2021).

At the individual level, on top of economic incentives and career development, factors like work-life balance (Asis & Carandang, 2020), effectiveness of communication among healthcare professionals with a diverse range of ethnicity (Olt et al., 2014), cultural differences, language barriers, avoidance of racial discriminations, integration into communities, access to professional development (Pressley et al., 2022), etc., may also be determinants influencing the longer-term retention of migrant healthcare professionals. A further point noteworthy is the deskilling of healthcare professionals in migration (Kurniati et al., 2017). Canada, for instance, is a signatory to the WHO Code but its failure to absorb healthcare professional immigrants into its healthcare systems has posed an ethical issue (Walton-Roberts, 2022), where foreign-trained registered nurses were required to work as domestic workers for two years before they could be registered as nurses (Salami, 2016). Pratt (1999) described this phenomenon vividly as "from registered nurse to registered nanny".

Professional Substitution

In healthcare, doctors were metaphorised as a "captain of the ship" (King et al., 1988). To conform to such a metaphorical mindset was the perceived position of nurses as "doctors' handmaidens" (Chen et al., 2023). Back to the early 1800s, a hospital doctor used the term "menial" synonymously as nurses (Helmstadter, 2008). More than 100 years afterwards, two authors wrote in a journal article published in 1945,

> IT IS THE INTENT [*sic*] of the writers to appraise the status of nursing as a profession … Nursing should extend and accelerate the present movement toward the organi[s]ation of collegiate schools, in order to advance the education of nurses to the level of the education of practitioners in the other professions."
>
> (Bixler & Bixler, 1945, pp. 730 & 735)

The contemporary healthcare workforce shortage has changed the dynamics. A study involving 161 hospitals across nine countries recruited hospital staff participants who treated patients suffering from breast cancer and acute myocardial infarction and it revealed that following nurses' further specialised education and training, they had shared most tasks with doctors (Maier et al., 2018). This change is not confined to doctors and nurses, but among healthcare professionals as well under the umbrella of professional substitution.

Professional substitution is one of the reforms to tackle healthcare manpower deficiencies, which refers to healthcare work being taken up by a profession from another profession through the transition of complete role or the transfer of tasks (Marks et al., 2017). It may take different modes, for instance, between doctors and other health professionals (e.g. specialists and general practitioners, doctors and nurses) and between health professionals and para-professionals (e.g. registered nurses and enrolled nurses/nursing assistants, allied health professionals and allied health assistants) (Duckett, 2005). Practical examples include nurses substituting doctors in maternity care for low-risk expectant mothers (Sutcliffe et al., 2012) and in primary care (Laurant et al., 2005), as well as physiotherapists as an alternative to doctors to manage patients with common musculoskeletal disorders (Marks et al., 2017).

Medico-legal measures and risks are inherent in professional substitution. In Canada, for example, nurses serving in community health institutes are allowed to provide and administer controlled substances to patients under certain restrictions in accordance with section 56(1) of the Controlled Drugs and Substances Act (Government of Canada, 2019). Similar but not identical statutory authorisations for nurses to administer scheduled medicines are also observed in other jurisdictions, such as Victoria of Australia (Department of Health of Victoria, 2022) and Washington State of the United States (Washington State Department of Health, n.d.). In addition to statutory controls, supervisors (e.g. physicians) in a professional substitution have to ensure appropriate measures in place to select or employ competent supervisees (e.g. physician assistants) and to provide necessary supervision in daily operations, so as to minimise, if not eliminate, the risk of alleged negligence and vicarious liability (Gore, 2000). To make efficient use of manpower and reduce the impact of insufficient skilled workforce, the WHO (2008) suggested a rational task-shifting approach to allocate appropriate tasks from healthcare professionals to others with less training. In view of the possible medico-legal liabilities, volunteering may not be a suitable strategy to deal with the shortage of healthcare workforce, despite that "volunteering constitutes an enormous reservoir of skills, energy and local knowledge" (Executive Board of the United Nations Development Programme and of the United Nations Population Fund, 2002, paragraph 13).

Community Care

Community care refers to "services and support to help people with care needs to live as independently as possible in their communities" (World Health Organization, 2004, p. 16). Governments of developed and developing jurisdictions, in principle, welcome community care as a common strategy to face modern healthcare challenges (Tong & Fong, 2018) and to manage the rising healthcare expenditure (Chappell et al., 2004). Careful planning is required in implementation of community care; or else, it may become "everybody's distant relative but nobody's baby" (Griffiths, 1988, p. iv). For example, policymakers generally believe that community care could help manage chronic patients and reduce their reliance on hospitals (Food and Health Bureau of Hong Kong, 2020), but a study in England reported otherwise that increase in community care may not necessarily lead to decrease in hospital expenses and activities (Lau et al., 2021).

There is no one-size-fits-all model of community care. In Europe, a survey covering six European countries found that policymakers had to take into consideration national and domestic factors in planning country-sensitive community care (Van Eenoo et al., 2016). In Singapore, research on a specialist-led general medicine model revealed that among other findings, coordination and communication between healthcare professionals from an acute hospital and other community care providers under study were not effective, and the latter were not well prepared to accept patients discharged from the former (Lai et al., 2021). In China, a study showed that community care had no impact on people's choice for ageing in place and the researchers proposed a shared-care model between family and the state, as it would be "particularly appropriate for China" (Zhou & Walker, 2021). In Hong Kong, the government has adopted "ageing in place as the core, institutional care as back-up" as the governing principle to manage the ageing population (Labour and Welfare Bureau & Social Welfare Department, Hong Kong, 2014) and planned to promote community care by establishing district health centres through medical-social collaboration (Chief Executive of Hong Kong, 2017) and made policy schemes for voluntary health insurance and elderly health vouchers through the private sector (Department of Health of Hong Kong, 2022; Health Bureau of Hong Kong, 2022a).

Increase in the Number of Places for Healthcare Students

To increase the number of places for healthcare students seems to be a simple answer to the shortage of healthcare professionals, but governments may not always be ready to pursue or commit this strategy, as it is very costly. It is not just about increasing the number of places at universities per se, but also relating to hiring sufficient number of teaching staff, making venues available for clinical training, ensuring enough work opportunities for new graduates and providing chances for subsequent continuous professional developments like specialty training for doctors (Michael et al., 2022).

The Rising Nationalism

International cooperation and government strategies with practical difficulties are discussed above, and there is no straightforward answer to deal with the global healthcare workforce shortage. The WHO (2006, p. xx) wrote,

> A blueprint approach will not work, as effective workforce strategies must be matched to a country's unique history and situation. Most workforce problems are deeply embedded in changing contexts, and they cannot be easily resolved. These problems can be emotionally charged because of status issues and politically loaded because of divergent interests. That is why workforce solutions require stakeholders to be engaged in both problem diagnosis and problem solving.

The quote above has rightly pointed out the importance to address political considerations, as political undercurrents have been in place to make healthcare workforce shortage a political agenda. The evolving nationalism is a further and real concern, as demonstrated in the WHO's failure in restructuring a sharing culture against the vaccine nationalism of developed countries to enhance poor global villagers' equitable access to vaccines and treatments (Eccleston-Turner & Upton, 2021) through COVAX, with a full title of "COVID-19 Vaccines Global Access" (World Health Organization, 2022a). Both developed and developing countries understand the seriousness of healthcare workforce challenges well, but they may only be looking for some quick solutions under the context of nationalism, as penned in the abstract of Britnell's book (2019),

> No country today manages its health workforce and workforce needs particularly well. Neither rich nor poor countries are prepared to tackle the problems facing their health workforce, even though many analyse and outline the coming shortages. Countries

and organi[s]ations often try to spend their way out of problems with short-term fixes, causing more problems for others and, ultimately, themselves.

For instance, Chakravorty et al. (2021) predicted that the NHS still needs "migrant health professionals now and will do so for generations to come" in post-Brexit United Kingdom to fill the several-thousand vacancies of doctors and more than 100,000 posts of nurses. The rise of nationalism has also influenced medical training, where the anti-global political mindset has put global health education under threat, which allows medical students to practise clinical work in societies with demography, socioeconomic statuses and cultures different from their home countries (Peluso et al., 2019). Furthermore, a survey in Nova Scotia of Canada published that foreign-trained healthcare nurses with temporary work permits were subject to the local communities' racist attitudes and treatments, and the researcher argued that such observations must be examined under the context of political economy (Nourpanah, 2019).

Conclusion

SDG 3 of the 2030 Agenda addresses, among others, the needs for universal health coverage, increasing healthcare financing, and the sustainable supply of healthcare workforce especially in least developed and small-island developing countries (United Nations Development Programme, 2022), where the availability of healthcare workforce is the key to success in the goal attainment. Strategies discussed above are like double-edged knives, all with their strengths and weaknesses. At the global level, to fix the global workforce shortage through international cooperation sounds like a utopia, as exemplified by the member states' ad hoc and ineffective implementations of the WHO Code. At the national level, telehealth and healthcare technologies could help save manpower to a certain extent, but from the viewpoint of holistic care, they could not replace the labour-intensive and high-touch care for patients before they are transformed into a "re-humanised" status (Shelley, 2016). Recruitment of foreign-trained healthcare professionals seems to be a fast solution, but it has also created more issues like brain drain in source countries and cultural if not racial conflicts in destination countries. Professional substitution is not risk-free in terms of medico-legal liabilities and it needs rational and careful planning. Community care is country-specific in the context and may not be generalised and duplicated easily for the use in other jurisdictions. It is costly to increase the number of places of healthcare students. To further exert immense pressure to the issue of insufficient supply of healthcare professionals is the rising nationalism, which makes international cooperation more complex.

How could governments react to the present complexity? In response to a query of mass media on the reintroduction of a government cap on the number of places of medical and dentist students, James Cleverly, the former Secretary of State for Education of the United Kingdom, replied in August 2022, 'you can't just "flick a switch" to increase the capacity to train more doctors' (Government defends medical student number cap, 2022). This reply fits well with a Chinese proverb, saying, "Water far away cannot put out a fire nearby", but there is no excuse for not doing long-term strategies for the future, as the issues of healthcare workforce shortage have been decades-old. Could a government tell people when it would flick such a switch or other necessary switches? Governments' preference for quick fixes will not help the longer-term, not to say the long-term, planning to survive the workforce challenges. It is true that it is not easy to manage healthcare workforce shortage. However, it needs love and political courage for governments to make longer- and long-term strategies to protect people's right to health through a sustainable pool of healthcare professionals, not only within their jurisdictions but in the globe as envisaged in SDG 3. Another Chinese proverb does its best as a concluding remark for this chapter, "A journey of a thousand miles begins with a single step".

References

Adhanom Ghebreyesus, T. (2020, December 2). *Opening.* World Policy Conference 2020. https://www.worldpolicyconference.com/wp-content/uploads/2020-proceedings-pdf/en/2.opening_tedros.pdf

Aluttis, C., Bishaw, T., & Frank, M. W. (2014). The workforce for health in a globalized context – Global shortages and international migration. *Global Health Action, 7*(1), Article 23611. https://doi.org/10.3402/gha.v7.23611

American Hospital Association. (2022). *Massive growth in expenses and rising inflation fuel continued financial challenges for America's hospitals and health systems.* https://www.aha.org/system/files/media/file/2022/04/2022-Hospital-Expenses-Increase-Report-Final-Final.pdf

Asis, E., & Carandang, R. R. (2020). The plight of migrant care workers in Japan: A qualitative study of their stressors on caregiving. *Journal of Migration and Health, 1–2*, Article 100001. https://doi.org/10.1016/j.jmh.2020.100001

60   *Kar-wai Tong*

Astin, F. (2018). Do patients take angioplasty seriously? *European Journal of Cardiovascular Nursing, 17*(3), 194–195. https://doi.org/10.1177/147451 5117737767

Bixler, G. K., & Bixler, R. W. (1945). The professional status of nursing. *The American Journal of Nursing, 45*(9), 730–735.

Bludau, H. (2021). Global healthcare worker migration. *Oxford Research Encyclopedia of Anthropology*, online publication. https://doi.org/10.1093/acrefore/9780190854584.013.231

Britnell, M. (2019). *Human: Solving the global workforce crisis in healthcare.* Oxford University Press. https://doi.org/10.1093/oso/9780198836520.001.0001

Buchan, J., & Campbell, J. (2013). Challenges posed by the global crisis in the health workforce: No workforce, no health. *British Medical Journal, 347*, Article f6201. https://doi.org/10.1136/bmj.f6201

Buchan, J., & Poz, M. R. (2003). Role definitions, skill mix, multi-skilling and "new" workers. *Studies in HSO&P, 21*, 275–300.

Campbell, J., Dussault, G., Buchan, J., Pozo-Martin, F., Guerra Arias, M., Leone, C., Siyam, A., & Cometto, G. (2013). *A universal truth: No health without a workforce.* Forum Report, Third Global Forum on Human Resources for Health, Recife, Brazil. Geneva, Global Health Workforce Alliance and World Health Organization. https://cdn.who.int/media/docs/default-source/health-workforce/ghwn/ghwa/ghwa_auniversaltruthreport.pdf?sfvrsn=966aa7ab_3&download=true

Chakravorty, I., Bamrah, J. S., & Mehta, R. (2021). Migration of healthcare professionals in post-Brexit Britain. *The Physician, 6*(3), 1–8. https://doi.org/10.38192/1.6.3.15

Chappell, N. L., Dlitt, B. H., Hollander, M. J., Miller, J. A., & McWilliam, C. (2004). Comparative costs of home care and residential care. *The Gerontologist, 44*(3), 389–400. https://doi.org/10.1093/geront/44.3.389

Chen, J., Leung, G. K. K., & Tong, K.-w. (2023). Relationship with colleagues. In J. S. P. Chiu, A. Lee, & K.-w. Tong (Eds.), *Healthcare law and ethics: Principles & practices.* City University of Hong Kong.

Chen, W. H., Shen, L. J., Guan, R. J., & Wu, F. L. L. (2013). Assessment of an automatic robotic arm for dispensing of chemotherapy in a 2500-bed medical center. *Journal of the Formosan Medical Association, 112*(4), 193–200. https://doi.org/10.1016/j.jfma.2011.11.026

Chief Executive of Hong Kong. (2017). *The chief executive's 2017 policy address: We connect for hope and happiness.* https://www.policyaddress.gov.hk/2017/eng/pdf/PA2017.pdf

Chikhaoui, E., Alajmi, A., & Larabi-Marie-Sainte, S. (2022). Artificial intelligence applications in healthcare sector: Ethical and legal challenges. *Emerging Science Journal, 6*(4), 717–738. https://doi.org/10.28991/ESJ-2022-06-04-05

Davenport, T., & Kalakota, R. (2019). The potential for artificial intelligence in healthcare. *Future Healthcare Journal, 6*(2), 94–98. https://doi.org/10.7861/futurehosp.6-2-94

Department of Health of Hong Kong. (2022). *Health care voucher: About the scheme.* https://www.hcv.gov.hk/en/index.html

Department of Health of Victoria. (2022). *Nurses and midwives.* https://www.health.vic.gov.au/drugs-and-poisons/nurses-and-midwives

Duckett, S. J. (2005). Health workforce design for the 21st century. *Australian Health Review, 29*(2), 201–210. https://doi.org/10.1071/ah050201

Eccleston-Turner, M., & Upton, H. (2021). International collaboration to ensure equitable access to vaccines for COVID-19: The ACT-accelerator and the COVAX facility. *The Milbank Quarterly, 99*(2), 426–449. https://doi.org/10.1111/1468-0009.12503

Executive Board of the United Nations Development Programme and of the United Nations Population Fund. (2002). *United nations volunteers: Report of the administrator (DP/2002/18).* https://www.unv.org/sites/default/files/UNDP%20EB%20Report%20(DP%202002-18).pdf

Feld, S. (2021). Emigration of health personnel from developing countries. In S. Feld (Ed.), *International migration, remittances and brain drain* (pp. 49–76). *Demographic transformation and socio-economic development* (Vol. 13). Springer. https://doi.org/10.1007/978-3-030-75513-3_4

Food and Health Bureau of Hong Kong. (2008). *Your health your life: Healthcare reform consultation document.* https://www.healthbureau.gov.hk/beStrong/files/consultation/Condochealth_full_eng.pdf

Food and Health Bureau of Hong Kong. (2020). *Southern district council: District health centre in southern district (SDC Paper No. 34/2020).* https://www.districtcouncils.gov.hk/south/doc/2020_2023/en/dc_meetings_doc/17627/S_2020_34_EN.pdf

Gore, C. L. (2000). A physician's liability for mistakes of a physical assistant. *The Journal of Legal Medicine, 21*(1), 125–142. https://doi.org/10.1080/019476400272837

Government defends medical student number cap. (2022, August 18). *BBC news.* https://www.bbc.com/news/health-62594141

Government of Canada. (2019). *Subsection 56(1) class exemption for nurses providing health care at a community health facility.* https://www.canada.ca/en/health-canada/services/health-concerns/controlled-substances-precursor-chemicals/policy-regulations/policy-documents/subsection-56-exemption-nurses-providing-primary-care-community-health-facility.html

Griffiths, R. (1988). *Community care: Agenda for action – A report to the secretary of state for social services.* London: Her Majesty's Stationary Office.

Health Bureau of Hong Kong. (2022a). *About VHIS.* https://www.vhis.gov.hk/en/about_us/index.html

Health Bureau of Hong Kong. (2022b). *Medical registration (Amendment) Bill 2021.* https://www.healthbureau.gov.hk/en/press_and_publications/other-info/210500_amendments_mro/index.html

Health Bureau of Hong Kong. (2022c). *Statistics: Domestic health account.* https://www.healthbureau.gov.hk/statistics/en/dha/dha_summary_report.htm#A

Helmstadter, C. (2008). Authority and leadership: The evolution of nursing management in 19th century teaching hospitals. *Journal of Nursing Management, 16*(1), 4–13. https://doi.org/10.1111/j.1365-2934.2007.00811.x

Hospital Authority of Hong Kong. (2021). *Hospital authority annual report 2020–2021.* https://www.ha.org.hk/haho/ho/cc/HA_Annual_Report_2020-21_en.pdf

Howard-Jones, N. (1975). *The scientific background of the international sanitary conferences 1851–1938.* World Health Organization. http://whqlibdoc.who.int/publications/1975/14549_eng.pdf

King, N. M. P., Churchill, L. R., & Cross, A. W. (1988). *The physician as captain of the ship: A critical reappraisal.* Springer Dordrecht. https://doi.org/10.1007/978-0-585-27589-5

Kinney, E. D., & Clark, B. A. (2004). Provisions for health and health care in the constitutions of the countries of the world. *Cornell International Law Journal, 37*(2), 285–355. https://ssrn.com/abstract=687962

Kurniati, A., Chen, C.-M., Efendi, F., & Ogawa, R. (2017). A deskilling and challenging journey: The lived experience of Indonesian nurse returnees. *International Nursing Review, 64*(4), 494–501. https://doi.org/10.1111/inr.12352

Labour and Welfare Bureau, & Social Welfare Department, Hong Kong. (2014). *Home care and community support services for the elderly and persons with disabilities* (LC Paper No. CB(2)2077/13–14(05)). http://www.legco.gov.hk/yr13-14/english/panels/ws/papers/ws0725cb2-2077-5-e.pdf

Lai, Y. F., Lee, S. Y., Xiong, J., Leow, S. Y., Lim, C. W., & Ong, B. C. (2021). Challenges and opportunities in pragmatic implementation of a holistic hospital care model in Singapore: A mixed-method case study. *PLoS One, 16*(1), Article e0245650. https://doi.org/10.1371/journal.pone.0245650

Lau, Y. S., Malisauskaite, G., Brookes, N., Hussein, S., & Sutton, M. (2021). Complements or substitutes? Associations between volumes of care provided in the community and hospitals. *The European Journal of Health Economics, 22*(8), 1167–1181. https://doi.org/10.1007/s10198-021-01329-6

Laurant, M., van der Biezen, M., Wijers, N., Watananirun, K., Kontopantelis, E., & van Vught, A. J. A. H. (2018). Nurses as substitutes for doctors in primary care. *Cochrane Database of Systematic Reviews, 7*(7), Article CD001271. https://doi.org/10.1002/14651858.CD001271.pub3

Lee, T., Propper, C., & Stoye, G. (2019). Medical labour supply and the production of healthcare. *Fiscal Studies, 40*(4), 621–661. https://doi.org/10.1111/1475-5890.12198

Liao, Y. H., Lin, T. Y., Wu, C. C., & Shih, Y. N. (2021). Can occupational therapy manpower be replaced with social robots in a singing group during COVID-19? *Work, 68*(1), 21–26. https://doi.org/10.3233/WOR-205096

Liu, E. & Yue, S. Y. (1998). *Health care expenditure and financing in Hong Kong.* Research and Library Services Division, Provisional Legislative Council Secretariat. https://www.legco.gov.hk/yr97-98/english/sec/library/06plc.pdf

Loh, P. K., Sabesan, S., Allen, D., Caldwell, P., Mozer, R., Komesaroff, P. A., Talman, P., Williams, M., Shaheen, N., Grabinski, O., & Withnall, D., on behalf of The Royal Australasian College of Physicians Telehealth Working Group. (2013). Practical aspects of telehealth: Financial considerations. *Internal Medicine Journal, 43*(7), 829–834. https://doi.org/10.1111/imj.12193

Magennis, P., Begley, A., Dhariwal, D. K., Smith, A., & Hutchison, I. (2022). Oral and maxillofacial surgery (OMFS) consultant workforce in the UK: Reducing consultant numbers resulting from recruitment issues, pension pressures, changing job-plans, and demographics when combined with the COVID backlog in elective surgery, requires urgent action. *British Journal of Oral and Maxillofacial Surgery, 60*(1), 14–19. https://doi.org/10.1016/j.bjoms.2021.10.011

Maier, C. B., Köppen, J., Busse, R., & MUNROS team. (2018). Task shifting between physicians and nurses in acute care hospitals: Cross-sectional study in nine countries. *Human Resources for Health, 16*, Article 24. https://doi.org/10.1186/s12960-018-0285-9

Marks, D., Comans, T., Bisset, L., & Scuffham, P. A. (2017). Substitution of doctors with physiotherapists in the management of common musculoskeletal disorders: A systematic review. *Physiotherapy, 103*(4), 341–351. https://doi.org/10.1016/j.physio.2016.11.006

McPake, B., Maeda, A., Araújo, E. C., Lemiere, C., El Maghraby, A., & Cometto, G. (2013). Why do health labour market forces matter? *Bulletin of the World Health Organization, 91*(11), 841–846. https://doi.org/10.2471/BLT.13.118794

Michael, S. G., Reynolds, W., & Michael, K. (2020). Re: Medical school places: What will be the effect of lifting the cap? *British Medical Journal, 370*, Article m3358. https://doi.org/10.1136/bmj.m3358

Nourpanah, S. (2019). "Maybe we shouldn't laugh so loud": The hostility and welcome experienced by foreign nurses on temporary work permits in Nova Scotia, Canada. *Labour / Le Travail, 83*(Spring), 105–120. https://doi.org/10.1353/llt.2019.0004

Olt, H., Jirwe, M., Saboonchi, F., Gerrish, K., & Azita Emami, A. (2014). Communication and equality in elderly care settings: Perceptions of first- and second-generation immigrant and native Swedish healthcare workers. *Diversity and Equality in Health and Care, 11*(2), 99–111. https://doi.org/10.21767/2049-5471.10008

Peluso, M. J., DeLuca, M. A., Dagna, L., Garg, B., Hafler, J. P., Kiguli-Malwadde, E., Mayanja-Kizza, H., Maley, M. A., & Rohrbaugh, R. M. (2019). Socially accountable global health education amidst political uncertainty and reactionary nationalism: A value proposition and recommendations for action. *Annals of Global Health, 85*(1), 118. https://doi.org/10.5334/aogh.2569

Portela, G. Z., Fehn, A. C., Ungerer, R. L. S., & Poz, M. R. D. (2017). Human resources for health: Global crisis and international cooperation. *Ciência & Saúde Coletiva, 22*(7), 2237–2246. https://doi.org/10.1590/1413-81232017227.02702017

64   *Kar-wai Tong*

Pratt, G. (1999). From registered nurse to registered nanny: Discursive geographies of Filipina domestic workers in Vancouver, British Columbia. *Economic Geography, 75*(3), 215–236. https://doi.org/10.1111/j.1944-8287.1999.tb00077.x

Pressley, C., Newton, D., Garside, J., Simkhada, P., & Simkhada, B. (2022). Global migration and factors that support acculturation and retention of international nurses: A systematic review. *International Journal of Nursing Studies Advances, 4*, Article 100083. https://doi.org/10.1016/j.ijnsa.2022.100083

Ramadhan, A. P., & Santoso, D. (2015). Health workers absenteeism: Indonesia urban public health centres. *Journal of Public Health, 23*(3), 165–173. https://doi.org/10.1007/s10389-015-0667-6

Research Office of the Legislative Council Secretariat of Hong Kong. (2019). *Information note: Admission of overseas-trained doctors in Singapore and Australia (IN13/18–19).* https://www.legco.gov.hk/research-publications/english/1819in13-admission-of-overseas-trained-doctors-in-singapore-and-australia-20190509-e.pdf

Salami, B. (2016). Migrant nurses and federal caregiver programs in Canada: Migration and health human resources paradox. *Canadian Journal of Nursing Research, 48*(2), 35–40. https://doi.org/10.1177/0844562116663951

Shelley, B. P. (2016). Re-humanizing "high-tech, no touch" medicine: Narrative medicine and cinemeducation perspectives. *Archives of Medicine and Health Sciences, 4*(1), 1–5. https://doi.org/10.4103/2321-4848.183367

Sutcliffe, K., Caird, J., Kavanagh, J., Rees, R., Oliver, K., Dickson, K., Woodman, J., Barnett-Paige, E., & Thomas, J. (2012). Comparing midwife-led and doctor-led maternity care: A systematic review of reviews. *Journal of Advanced Nursing, 68*(11), 2376–2386. https://doi.org/10.1111/j.1365-2648.2012.05998.x

Tankwanchi, A. B., Vermund, S. H., & Perkins, D. D. (2014). Has the WHO Global Code of Practice on the International Recruitment of Health Personnel been effective?. *The Lancet Global Health, 2*(7), e390-e391. https://doi.org/10.1016/S2214-109X(14)70240-2

The Government of the Hong Kong Special Administrative Region. (2021, October 21). *Hospital authority welcomes passage of medical registration (amendment) bill 2021 at legislative council* [Press release]. https://www.info.gov.hk/gia/general/202110/21/P2021102100473.htm

The King's Fund. (2022). *Key facts and figures about the NHS.* https://www.kingsfund.org.uk/audio-video/key-facts-figures-nhs

Thomson, S., Figueras, J., Evetovits, T., Jowett, M., Mladovsky, P., Maresso, A., Cylus, J., Karanikolos, M., & Kluge, H. (2014). *Economic crisis, health systems and health in Europe: Impact and implications for policy.* World Health Organization Regional Office for Europe. https://www.euro.who.int/__data/assets/pdf_file/0008/257579/Economic-crisis-health-systems-Europe-impact-implications-policy.pdf

Tobin, J. (2012). *The right to health in international law.* Oxford University Press. https://doi.org/10.1093/acprof:oso/9780199603299.001.0001

Tong, K.-w. & Fong, K. N. K. (2018). Community-based rehabilitation in Hong Kong: Opportunities and future challenges. In B. Fong, A. Ng, & P. Yuen (Eds.), *Sustainable health and long-term care solutions for an aging population* (pp. 294–319). IGI Global. https://doi.org/10.4018/978-1-5225-2633-9.ch016

United Nations Committee on Economic, Social and Cultural Rights of the Economic and Social Council. (2000). *General comment No. 14 (2000) on substantive issues arising in the implementation of the international covenant on economic, social and cultural rights (E/C.12/2000/4, CESCR general comment 14).* https://digitallibrary.un.org/record/425041

United Nations Development Programme. (2022). *The SDGs in action.* https://www.undp.org/sustainable-development-goals

Van Eenoo, L., Declercq, A., Onder, G., Finne-Soveri, H., Garms-Homolová, V., Jónsson, P. V., Dix, O. H. M., Smit, J. H., van Hout, H. P. J., & van der Roest, H. G. (2016). Substantial between-country differences in organising community care for older people in Europe—A review. *European Journal of Public Health, 26*(2), 213–219. https://doi.org/10.1093/eurpub/ckv152

Wade, V. A., Karnon, J., Elshaug, A. G., & Hiller, J. E. (2010). A systematic review of economic analyses of telehealth services using real time video communication. *BMC Health Services Research, 10*, Article 233. https://doi.org/10.1186/1472-6963-10-233

Walton-Roberts, M. (2022). The ethics of recruiting foreign-trained healthcare workers. *Healthcare Management Forum, 35*(4), 248–251. https://doi.org/10.1177/08404704221095129

Washington State Department of Health. (n.d.). *Who can prescribe and administer prescriptions in Washington State.* https://doh.wa.gov/licenses-permits-and-certificates/facilities-z/pharmacies/who-can-prescribe-and-administer-prescriptions-washington-state

World Health Organization. (1946). *Constitution of the world health organization.* https://apps.who.int/gb/bd/PDF/bd47/EN/constitution-en.pdf

World Health Organization. (1986). *Ottawa charter for health promotion, 1986.* https://www.euro.who.int/__data/assets/pdf_file/0004/129532/Ottawa_Charter.pdf

World Health Organization. (2004). *A glossary of terms for community health care and services for older persons.* WHO Centre for Health Development: Ageing and Health Technical Report, Volume 5 (WHO/WKC/Tech. Ser./04.2). https://apps.who.int/iris/bitstream/handle/10665/68896/WHO_WKC_Tech.Ser._04.2.pdf?sequence=1&isAllowed=y

World Health Organization. (2005). *Sustainable health financing, universal coverage and social health insurance* (WHA 58.33). http://apps.who.int/iris/bitstream/10665/20383/1/WHA58_33-en.pdf?ua=1

World Health Organization. (2006). *The world health report 2006 – Working together for health.* https://apps.who.int/iris/bitstream/handle/10665/43432/9241563176_eng.pdf?sequence=1&isAllowed=y

World Health Organization. (2008). *Task shifting: Rational redistribution of tasks among health workforce teams. Global recommendations and guidelines.* Geneva: Author. https://apps.who.int/iris/bitstream/handle/10665/43821/9789241596312_eng.pdf

World Health Organization. (2010). *WHO global code of practice on the international recruitment of health personnel.* https://www.un.org/en/development/desa/population/migration/generalassembly/docs/globalcompact/WHA_RES_63.16.pdf

World Health Organization. (2011). *Health workforce strengthening.* https://apps.who.int/gb/ebwha/pdf_files/WHA64/A64_R6-en.pdf

World Health Organization. (2016). *Global strategy on human resources for health: Workforce 2030.* https://apps.who.int/iris/bitstream/handle/10665/250368/9789241511131-eng.pdf?sequence=1&isAllowed=y

World Health Organization. (2018, February 22). *Health inequities and their causes.* https://www.who.int/news-room/facts-in-pictures/detail/health-inequities-and-their-causes

World Health Organization. (2019, February 20). *Countries are spending more on health, but people are still paying too much out of their own pockets.* https://www.who.int/news/item/20-02-2019-countries-are-spending-more-on-health-but-people-are-still-paying-too-much-out-of-their-own-pockets

World Health Organization. (2020). *Report of the WHO expert advisory group on the relevance and effectiveness of the WHO global code of practice on the international recruitment of health personnel: Report by the Director-General (A73/9).* https://apps.who.int/gb/ebwha/pdf_files/WHA73/A73_9-en.pdf

World Health Organization. (2021). *Health workforce support and safeguards list, 2020.* https://cdn.who.int/media/docs/default-source/health-workforce/hwf-support-and-safeguards-list8jan.pdf?sfvrsn=1a16bc6f_14

World Health Organization. (2022a) *COVAX: Working for global equitable access to COVID-19 vaccines.* https://www.who.int/initiatives/act-accelerator/covax

World Health Organization. (2022b). *Social determinants of health.* https://www.who.int/health-topics/social-determinants-of-health#tab=tab_1

World Health Organization. (2022c). *The global health workforce alliance mandate completed.* https://www.who.int/teams/health-workforce/workforcealliance

World Health Organization. (2022d). *World health statistics 2022: Monitoring health for the SDGs, sustainable development goals.* https://apps.who.int/iris/rest/bitstreams/1435584/retrieve

World Health Organization Regional Office for Europe. (2021). *Health and well-being and the 2030 Agenda for Sustainable Development in the WHO European Region: An analysis of policy development and implementation.* https://apps.who.int/iris/bitstream/handle/10665/339795/WHO-EURO-2021-1878-41629-56873-eng.pdf

Wu, K. F., Hu, J. L., & Chiou, H. (2021). Degrees of shortage and uncovered ratios for long-term care in Taiwan's regions: Evidence from dynamic DEA. *International Journal of Environmental Research and Public Health, 18*(2), Article 605. https://doi.org/10.3390/ijerph18020605

Zakus, D., & Cortinois, A. A. (2002). Primary healthcare and community participation: Origins, implementation, and the future. In B. J. Fried & L. M. Gaydos (Eds.), *World health systems: Challenges and perspectives* (pp. 39–54). Health Administration Press.

Zhou, J., & Walker, A. (2021). The impact of community care services on the preference for ageing in place in urban China. *Health and Social Care Community*, *29*(4), 1041–1050. https://doi.org/10.1111/hsc.13138

5   Management Strategies in Information System, Technology Adoption and Medical Products for Community Health

Fowie Ng

Introduction

The United Nations Sustainable Development Goals (SDGs) are the 17 goals with 169 targets to be achieved by the year 2030. These targets were agreed upon by world leaders from 191 United Nations Member States in September 2015. In relation to health, SDG 3 advocates for all nations to ensure healthy lives and promote well-being for all of different ages and backgrounds (World Health Organization, n.d.b). With such complexity in different health systems around the world, there is an urgent need for health ministers, government representatives and other stakeholders at local, regional and international levels to collaborate within the arena of Public Health domains. The common agenda is to improve the health and well-being of their citizens regarding the implementation and achievement of the 13 targets of SDG 3. The recent outbreak of COVID-19 across the globe has further accelerated the need for a concerted approach to fighting the pandemic through better management strategies with connected information systems using the latest technology and medical products such as vaccines and drugs in an attempt to protect the citizens and the economy of the societies.

Health of the Nations

The global average life expectancy at birth for both sexes is 73 years in the year 2020. There was a wide range of differences between life expectancy across periods within a country as well as between countries, especially in relation to the development status of the countries or localities. For example, Haiti's life expectancy for males was 27.97 years and females 35.37 years in 2010. It has risen to 63.34 years for males and 64.76 years for females (The Global Health Observatory,

DOI: 10.4324/9781003305637-5

2022). To the other extreme, Hong Kong has consistently ranked top in the life expectancy of males and females since 2013 (Na, 2022). The life expectancies at birth have been raising to 83.0 years for males and 87.7 years for females in 2021 (Centre for Health Protection, 2022). In trying to understand why Hong Kong has enjoyed such longevity, recent research studies have highlighted some factors and frameworks for other localities to replicate through deliberate policies among developing and developed countries. Chung and Marmot (2020) explained some possible factors why the population in Hong Kong has the longest life expectancy in the world in such a densely populated city. The key contributing components are the:

> non-Western diet; the physical and built environment where public transportation, sports centers, grocery stores, shops that sell commodities of basic living, and private health care clinics are readily available; the geographical location with subtropical climate that does not give rise to frequent extreme weather; and the existence of a public health care system that gives people adequate health care, regardless of lack of means.
>
> (para. 4)

Another study investigated the comparison of factors behind Hong Kong's survival advantage over both long-living, and high-income countries. The leading longevity enjoyed by Hong Kong citizens is the result of fewer diseases of poverty while suppressing the diseases of affluence. The mortality rate is lower from cardiovascular diseases for both sexes and cancer for females as well as transport accidents for males. This is further reinforced by a combination of economic prosperity and low levels of smoking after years of work on anti-smoking initiatives in society (Ni et al., 2021). The reasons for Hong Kong's longest life expectancy can now be understood by the adoption of healthier lifestyles and the city's well-developed infrastructure that provided easy access to health, food and social services in a concert effort to improve the health of the nation. This coincides with several targets of SDG 3 such as the SDG 3.6 about road traffic injuries, SDG 3.8 about universal health coverage and SDG 3.a about tobacco control. The public health framework can be employed as the backbone to understand the SDGs. Griffiths et al. (2005) outlined a conceptual model for public health practice. It consists of three key domains of public health, namely the health improvement domain, health protection domain as well as health service delivery and quality (Griffiths et al., 2005). This model was further adopted in developing the first

Figure 5.1 Simplified Public Health Domains (adapted from Griffiths et al., 2005).

Bachelor degree programme in public health in Hong Kong (Griffiths et al., 2009). As we can see in Figure 5.1, the health of the nation can be improved through the integration of the three domains and facilitated by good management strategies of information systems, technology adoption and medical products in the society.

Information Systems

The existing information systems among countries in health services should be reviewed so as to enlarge the scope in line with the SDG agenda. According to Nabyonga-Orem (2017), the monitoring requirements of information systems should be strengthened to produce relevant and reliable data which is timely and of good quality for further analysis. Apart from public sector, the private sector also plays a significant role in the delivery of health services. Hence, the interface and the interoperability of information systems are of paramount importance. The digital transformation of the global economy is a continuous process and has evolved from web 0.0 to web 1.0, web 2.0, web 3.0, web 4.0 and even web 5.0, respectively (Flat World Business, 2022). From a historical point of view, the birth of the internet in the 1990s signified the web 1.0 with a static read-only web. Web 2.0 encourages cooperation and assists in gathering collective intelligence for more flexible web design. Web 3.0 semantic web enhances the creating, sharing and connecting of materials through searching and analysing of words. The current web 4.0 is related to the mobile web in a connected society with different information systems and mobile connections with ubiquitous devices. The web 5.0 is also called the emotional web with the goal to create computers that can communicate with humans. It is claimed that Japan aspires to be the first nation to form a human-centred society so that everyone can live a healthy and active life (Shukla, 2022).

To facilitate the achievement of SDG 3, the healthcare systems needed to be digitalised. The evolution of patient record systems reflected the importance and scope of this transformation. The basic format is to transit the paper-based system to electronic medical record systems (EMR) for storing of clinical records only. The electronic health records (EHR) include other provider recorders related to the patients. The better approach is to develop patient health records (PHR) to include personal health information as well. Such a model is represented in Figure 5.2:

A minimum data set (MDS) is planned in each of the chosen systems to form the backbone for what sort of data to be collected and for analysis. This varies between different settings such as actual sectors in hospitals or primary care clinics. Some governments will set up mandatory standards for collecting essential data to provide health information for further planning and analysis. For example, Musa et al. (2022) revealed the uptake and use of MDS for older adults in care homes. They concluded that the uptake and use of MDS can enable all staff members to learn with each other in the team about the important issues for the caring of their residents. Furthermore, MDS is useful for future commissioning, planning as well as analysis with the use of digital technology. Every health-related facility needs to have formalised systems of records that are systematically

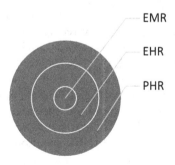

Figure 5.2 Simplified model of digital transformation of patient record systems (adapted from Heart et al., 2017; Househ et al., 2014).

organised, safe and readily accessible. Despite the advocation of electronic records, some institutions are still using both manual and electronic record systems. Such hybrid record systems can be performed effectively through the collaboration between clinical and administrative staff.

The SDG 3.8 target is to achieve universal health coverage, including financial risk protection with access to quality essential healthcare and access to safe, effective, quality and affordable essential medicines and vaccines for all (United Nations, 2022). The experiences of Hong Kong and Australia can demonstrate as examples of the use of information systems related to PHR to facilitate the achievement of universal health coverage as advocated by SDG 3.8. In Hong Kong, the territory-wide Electronic Health Record Sharing System (eHRSS) is the major electronic health record system developed by the Government for all members of the public (Ng et al., 2022). This is a lifelong electronic health record free for individual and family members to enable authorised healthcare providers to enhance continuity of care as well as integration of different healthcare services in both the public and private sectors. Although the registration is voluntary, the eHRSS and its associated app 'eHealth' users have already exceeded 4 million and 1.2 million (out of some 7.8 million population), respectively, by August 2021 (The Government of the Hong Kong Special Administrative Region, 2021). In addition to the users' medical data from inputs by authorised healthcare professionals, the eHealth App has added new functions since July 2021 to allow users to easily record their daily blood pressure, and blood sugar levels into the Apps to reinforce the primary care and the prevention of chronic diseases by managing their health anytime and anywhere by a 'click'. To combat COVID-19 of the policy of vaccines for all, vaccination records are stored electronically in eHealth app. Users can simply click the icon in 'Vaccines' to show the COVID-19 vaccination record or medical exemption certificate and recovery record QR codes easily. Family members' COVID-19 vaccination records can be added to their major carer's App too (eHealth, 2022).

Hong Kong is a metropolitan city with a merger of Eastern and Western cultures. Similarly, the use of Western medicine and Chinese medicine (CM) is very common in this special administrative region. At the primary care level of Chinese medicine in Hong Kong, there is a big leap step for the digital transformation of the Chinese medicine clinical management system. The recent Chinese Medicine Information System On-ramp called 'EC Connect' was rolled out in Hong Kong by the Electronic health record office. Chinese medicine clinics are invited to join and use at no cost so that they can access patients' online health records as well as share the patients' EHR with other practitioners. Apart from the daily administrative and clinical management functions of a clinic, one of the major features of the system is the adoption of standardised CM terminology to avoid misinterpretation. This system can be integrated into the current eHRSS system (eHealth, 2021).

In Australia, the 'My Health Record' let the citizens of Australia control their health information securely in one place and is available anywhere and anytime, especially during an emergency situation. Currently, some 23.3 million users have joined the digital initiative across the different states in Australia on an 'opt out' basis. Regarding providers, more than 99% of General Practitioners and Pharmacies, 97% of public hospitals and 23% of specialists have registered My Health Record (Australian Digital Health Agency, 2022). Similar to Hong Kong, vital information about COVID-19 vaccinations, boosters and test results are uploaded into the My Health Record which means users can access their information readily via their mobile devices by downloading an app whenever they need it.

Technology Adoption

The term 'Technology' in healthcare needs careful interpretation as sometimes it is always interpreted as computer or IT-related technology. The definition of healthcare technology can include any technology, including medical devices, information technology systems, algorithms, artificial intelligence (AI), cloud and blockchain, designed to support healthcare organisations (International Business Machines Corporation, n.d.). 'Innovation' and 'Technology' are often related buzzwords in the healthcare industry worldwide. Many countries especially low-income countries are facing constant and significant challenges to strive for the SDG 3 targets to ensure health and well-being for all at all ages. Many new opportunities are being emerged in the form of new innovative health technology, products, approaches and digital technologies. These are transforming the way how health data are collected and used locally and internationally to contribute to better health services. The global action plan for SDG 3 has indicated the need for stronger collaboration and better health (World Health Organization, 2019). Evidence-based innovations in healthcare technology are developed with collective action to be brought to scale such as point-of-care rapid diagnostic tests connected to mobile apps for screening and managing common non-communicable diseases (NCDs). Other examples of innovative technology can include heat-stable medicines and vaccines which do not need energy-consuming cold chain. Even with simple existing technology, the increased access and adoption of the pulse oximeter and contactless thermometers have contributed largely to the prevention and combat of COVID-19. During the COVID-19 pandemic, different countries such as Israel and China have adopted digital health passes or sometimes referred to as vaccine passports or vaccine certificates as a tool to allow the gradual reopening of the economy and travel from lockdown, quarantines, closure of business and stay-at-home requirements (Gostin et al., 2021).

Digital Health is also a very important phenomenon in the healthcare industry internationally. Indeed, the term 'Digital Health' is not a new concept in the healthcare industry. However, there is currently no universal agreement on the definition and the scope of the concept (Fatehi et al., 2020). Nevertheless, we can approach the concept by looking at the interpretation of the concept related to competencies regarding major stakeholders in the international arena. The international professional association Healthcare Information and Management Systems Society developed a blueprint for digital health advancement for healthcare providers around the world to apply the frameworks, models and tools for them to build, measure and advance health system transformation. Digital health has been defined as

> connects and empowers people and populations to manage health and wellness, augmented by accessible and supportive provider teams working within flexible, integrated, interoperable and digitally enabled care environments that strategically leverage digital tools, technologies and services to transform care delivery.
>
> (Healthcare Information and Management Systems
> Society, 2022)

World Health Organization (WHO) (2021) published the 'Global Strategy on Digital Health 2020–2025' to define the term as 'the field of knowledge and practice associated with the development and use of digital technologies to improve health (pg. 39)'. This definition by the WHO has expanded the initial concept of eHealth to include various digital consumers, with a wider range of gadgets such as smart devices and connected types of equipment to reinforce the discussion about innovation and technology for SDG 3. This Global Strategy on Digital Health has been adopted by the World Health Assembly in 2020 to provide the roadmap for member counties to improve health outcomes with the latest development in digital health and innovation (World Health Organization, 2021). Digital health also embraces other adoption of various digital technologies for healthcare. Many healthcare systems around the globe are developing or adopting the Internet of things, AI, big data and robotics.

Choun and Petre (2022) argued that patients must be empowered in the healthcare ecosystem during the current era with the exponential increase in the use of digital health as they are often left out of the innovation process. These patients or e-patients should be empowered to make informed decisions about their health status and diseases with adequate mastery of digital literacy and are willing to donate their data for research or clinical studies. Disruptive digital healthcare technology can help to shift the doctor-centred model of care to a patient-centred model of care to fit the targets of SDG 3. It also coincides with the emerging world of e-patients in 2004 in which they are the first generation of e-patients to start to use the internet to look for health information to have a different relationship with their doctors (Ferguson & Frydman, 2004).

Tin (2022) commented that COVID-19 has created the most favourable conditions ever for the global development of digital health. Evidence and ample examples from different countries have shown how information and digital health technology have contributed significantly and positively during the COVID-19 pandemic. For example, citizens in China and Singapore have witnessed a sharp increase in the adoption and implementation of tele-medicine, big data, geographical information systems, cloud computing, AI, instant messaging and wearable gadgets. A new model of 'internet + health' with internet hospitals has appeared in mainland China and is popular among patients in main China to get useful health information, second opinions as well as treatment (Ng, 2019). However, governments and health ministers need to have a responsive digital strategy with a strong governance structure that aimed for an integrated model of legal, finance and technology. A comprehensive digital health blueprint should be developed to provide universal health coverage facilitated by digital health technology. As the former Secretary of State for Health and Social Care of the United Kingdom announced, a plan for digital health and social care was set as the landmark document to show how the United Kingdom has made use of digital technology in health and social care and the further plan for the digital transformation across these two sectors (Department of Health and Social Care & NHS England, 2022).

Medical Products

By the year 2030, the SDG 3.4 and 3.8 targets of reducing one-third of the premature mortality for NCDs can be achieved through prevention and better treatment approach. Safe and affordable essential medicines and vaccines should be available to those who are in need. However, it is estimated that up to 2 billion people around the globe are lacking access to necessary medicines, vaccines, medical devices as well as other health products (World Health Organization, n.d.c). Cross-border shopping or prescription such as US citizens purchasing medicine in Mexico and parallel products are also filling the market due to relatively cheaper and readily accessible with the use of online shopping (Dalstrom et al., 2020). On the other extreme, substandard and falsified medical products emerged to address the gap in the market with great financial interest behind them. The gaps in the healthcare system have attracted the propping up of a dangerous, global and billion-dollar industry. It is estimated that nearly 80% of the drug to treat erectile dysfunction sold online is counterfeit (Fiouzi, n.d.). Hence, many of the branded anti-impotence drugs are found to be fake tablets in Hong Kong serving not only the customer in Hong Kong but also as the distribution centre for sending generic and fake pills all over the world (Lo, 2021). The complexity of the logistic supply chain and the manufacturing process have further reinforced the trade of substandard and falsified medical products. This is what WHO claimed to be one of the urgent health challenges in the coming decade in which one in ten medicines in low- and middle-income countries are substandard or falsified medical products such as medical medicines, vaccines, diagnostic devices and other health products. It happened not only for generic drugs but also for branded drugs no matter expensive products or inexpensive items.

The recent COVID-19 pandemic gave rise to an international race for biomedical and pharmaceutical firms to research and develop vaccines for COVID-19 for the benefit of mankind as well as for the financial performance of companies in especially those listed companies. Boseley (2021) analysed how the scientists at the University of Oxford have collaborated with a major giant pharmaceutical firm AstraZeneca listed in the stock market to launch a vaccine against the novel coronavirus, SARS-CoV-2, in less than a year. While some other COVID-19 vaccines are developed using a more traditional approach such as the CoronaVax by Sinovac produced in China was officially listed in the WHO Emergency Use Listing on 1 June 2021 (Sinovac, n.d.). The technology has been used traditionally in other vaccines and this time begins with collecting samples of COVID-19 viruses from infected people and then purifying and inactivating the virus (Mosley, 2020). Mallapaty (2021) has accounted that almost half of the 7.3 billion COVID-19 vaccines injected globally are from China's pharmaceutical companies. The collaboration between Ugur Sahin's team of BioNTech and Pfizer has made the impossible possible in nine months by using the technology of messenger RNA (mRNA) to create the COVID-19 vaccines (Bourla, 2022; Miller et al., 2022). Despite the work of various manufacturers to provide COVID-19 vaccines, only 67.7% of the world population has received at least one dose of the 12.58 billion doses administered in the world. Moreover, only 20.9% of the population in low-income countries have got one shot of the vaccine (Our World in Data, 2022). To revisit the SDG 3 targets of accessibility to medical products such as vaccines, the initiative of 'COVAX' was established in April 2000 with funding from govern-ments, donor organisations and self-financing member countries and was co-led by the Coalition for Epidemic Preparedness Innovations, Global Alliance for Vaccines and Immunisation and the WHO, along-side with the key delivery partner UNICEF to advocate the global collaboration in the acceleration of development, production and the equitable access to COVID-19 vaccines, tests and treatments (World Health Organization, n.d.a). Some 1.63 billion doses of COVID-19 vaccines have been delivered to 146 countries already of different brands or types of COVID-19 vaccines (Frackowiak et al., 2022). Yoo et al. (2022) evaluated the equity regarding the allocation and distri-bution of COVID-19 vaccines of COVAX based on the gross domestic product per capita. They concluded that COVAX is helping to balance the inequities globally but is not in a position enough to reverse the inequities in the delivery of the vaccines.

The pharmaceutical treatment options for COVID-19, two oral anti-viral drugs namely Pfizer's Paxloid and MSD's molnupiravir are cur-rently available and approved by FDA, respectively, for the treatment of COVID-19 cases (Gumbrecht et al., 2021). The clinical features of both drugs are to suppress the replication of the coronavirus and they should be prescribed within five days of the onset of the disease for patients with mild to moderate symptoms. Although there are inci-dents of rebound after taking the antiviral drugs, the reasons are still a mystery (Bregstein, 2022). In China including Hong Kong Special Administrative Region have other treatment options for using Chinese medicine widely during the waves of COVID-19. Three kinds of proprietary Chinese medicine are available as over-the-counter drugs, including "Lianhua Qingwen Jiaonang", "Jinhua Qinggan Keli" and "Huoxiang Zhengqi Pian" (Cheung, 2022). They are prescribed by Chinese medicine practitioners or simply purchase over the counter at local shops. Of course, it is strongly advisable to consult qualified Chinese medicine practitioners physically or even by telemedicine (Hong Kong Baptist University, 2022).

Conclusion

This chapter has started with a review of the three domains of Public Health to identify the three arenas of health improvement, health protection as well as health service delivery and quality for any healthcare system in the world. SDG 3 and the subcategories highlight the need to match the demand and provision of healthcare to all people to ensure healthy lives and promote well-being. While COVID-19 is threatening the previous decades of progress in global health, new mindsets and methods have to be applied to tackle the new normal or even the next normal. The increasing adoption of interoperability of health systems can reinforce the collection of essential data and the sharing of useful information for healthcare practitioners, health ministers locally, regionally and internationally. The digital transformation of the movement of digital health has been implemented and will continue to evolve in both low-income and high-income countries at different paces. Medical products including Western and Chinese medicine products of all kinds and costs will continue to be developed to provide evidence-based, effective, and value for money within the global village for all to access.

References

Australian Digital Health Agency. (2022). *Statistics and insights.* https://www.digitalhealth.gov.au/initiatives-and-programs/my-health-record/statistics

Boseley, S. (2021). The race to make a COVID-19 vaccine. *The Lancet,* *398*(10303), 832–833. https://doi.org/10.1016/S0140-6736(21)01902-4

Bourla, A. (2022). *Moonshot: Inside Pfizer's nine-month race to make the impossible possible.* Harper Business. https://www.harpercollins.com/products/moonshot-dr-albert-bourla?variant=39338844291106

Bregstein, J. (2022, August 2). Paxlovid rebound happens, though why and to whom are still a mystery. *STAT.* https://www.statnews.com/2022/08/02/paxlovid-rebound-mystery/

Centre for Health Protection. (2022). *Life expectancy at birth (male and female), 1971–2021.* https://www.chp.gov.hk/en/statistics/data/10/27/111.html

Cheung, E. (2022, March 16). Coronavirus: How do oral drugs molnupiravir and Paxlovid work, and what are other treatment options used in Hong Kong? *South China Morning Post*. https://www.scmp.com/news/hong-kong/health-environment/article/3170596/coronavirus-how-do-oral-drugs-molnupiravir-and

Choun, D., & Petre, A. (2022). *Digital health and patient data: Empowering patients in the healthcare ecosystem*. Routledge. https://doi.org/10.4324/9781003215868

Chung, R. Y. N., & Marmot, M. (2020). People in Hong Kong have the longest life expectancy in the world: Some possible explanations. *NAM Perspectives*. https://doi.org/10.31478/202001d

Dalstrom, M., Chung, R., & Castronovo, L. (2020). Impacting health through cross-border pharmaceutical purchases. *Medical Anthropology*, *39*(2), 182–195. https://doi.org/10.1080/01459740.2019.1642888

Department of Health and Social Care & NHS England. (2022). *A plan for digital health and social care*. https://www.gov.uk/government/publications/a-plan-for-digital-health-and-social-care/a-plan-for-digital-health-and-social-care

eHealth. (2021). *A step towards digitalisation – Rollout of the chinese medicine information system (CMIS) on-ramp*. https://www.ehealth.gov.hk/en/whats-new/ehealth-news/ehealth_news_21/cmis-on-ramp.php

eHealth. (2022). *Vaccine pass QR code*. https://www.portal.ehealth.gov.hk/app/covid19qr

Fatehi, F., Samadbeik, M., & Kazemi, A. (2020), What is digital health? Review of definitions. *Studies in Health Technology and Informatics*, *23*(275), 67–71. https://doi.org/10.3233/SHTI200696

Ferguson, T., & Frydman, G. (2004). The first generation of e-patients. *BMJ*, *328*, 1148–1149. https://doi.org/10.1136/bmj.328.7449.1148

Fiouzi, A. (n.d.). The other drug war: Inside the world of counterfeit Viagra. *MEL Magazine*. https://melmagazine.com/en-us/story/viagra-counterfeit-online

Flat World Business. (2022). *Digital evolution: Past, present and future outlook of digital technology*. https://flatworldbusiness.wordpress.com/digital-evolution/

Frackowiak, M., Pothitos, A., Lasocki, B., Triantafyllou, A., Jasiurska, A., & Gladun, E. (2022, September 2). Factbox: Vaccines delivered under COVAX sharing scheme for poorer countries. *Reuters*. https://www.reuters.com/business/healthcare-pharmaceuticals/vaccines-delivered-under-covax-sharing-scheme-poorer-countries-2022-01-03/

Gostin, L. O., Cohen, I. G., & Shaw, J. (2021). Digital health passes in the age of COVID-19: Are "vaccine passports" lawful and ethical? *JAMA*, *325*(19), 1933–1934. https://doi.org/10.1001/jama.2021.5283

Griffiths, S., Chor, J. S. Y., Yue, J., & Ng, F. (2009, April 27–May 1). *Multidisciplinary integration to public health training: Moving towards undergraduate public health education* [Conference presentation]. 12th

World Congress of Public Health, Istanbul, Turkey. https://wfpha.confex.
com/wfpha/2009/webprogram/Paper5417.html

Griffiths, S., Jewell, T., & Donnelly, P. (2005). Public health in practice: The
three domains of public health. *Public Health*, *119*(10), 907–913. https://doi.
org/10.1016/j.puhe.2005.01.010

Gumbrecht, J., Sealy, A., & Howard, J. (2021, December 24). FDA author-
izes second antiviral pill to treat Covid-19. *CNN*. https://edition.cnn.
com/2021/12/22/health/pfizer-antiviral-pill-authorized/index.html

Heart, T., Ben-Assuli, O., & Shabtai, I. (2017). A review of PHR, EMR and
EHR integration: A more personalized healthcare and public health policy. *Health Policy and Technology*, *6*(1), 20–25. https://doi.org/10.1016/j.
hlpt.2016.08.002

Healthcare Information and Management Systems Society. (2022).
What is digital health? https://www.himss.org/what-we-do-solutions/
digital-health-transformation

Hong Kong Baptist University. (2022, March 9). *HKBU fights against COVID-
19 with Chinese medicine and comprehensive care* [Press release]. https://
www.hkbu.edu.hk/en/whats-new/press-release/2022/0309-hkbu-fights-
against-covid-19-with-chinese-medicine-and-comprehensive-care.html

Househ, M. S., Borycki, E. M., Rohrer, W. M., & Kushniruk, A. W.
(2014). Developing a framework for meaningful use of personal health
records (PHRs). *Health Policy and Technology*, *3*(4), 272–280. https://doi.
org/10.1016/j.hlpt.2014.08.009

International Business Machines Corporation. (n.d.). *What is healthcare
technology?*. https://www.ibm.com/topics/healthcare-technology

Lo, C. (2021, October 25). Fake Viagra, Cialis tablets among Hong Kong's
record HK$55 million seizure of controlled pharmaceuticals. *South China
Morning Post*. https://www.scmp.com/news/hong-kong/law-and-crime/
article/3153528/fake-viagra-cialis-tablets-among-hong-kongs-record

Mallapaty, S. (2021, October 14). China's COVID vaccines have been crucial –
Now immunity is waning. *Nature News*. https://www.nature.com/articles/
d41586-021-02796-w

Miller, J., Türeci, Ö., & Sahin, U. (2022). The vaccine inside the race to con-
quer the Covid-19 pandemic. *St. Martin's Press*. https://us.macmillan.com/
books/9781250280367/the-vaccine

Mosley, M. (2020). *Covid-19: What you need to know about the coronavirus and
the race for the vaccine*. Short Books Ltd.

Musa, M. K., Akdur, G., Brand, S., Killett, A., Spilsbury, K., Peryer, G.,
Burton, J. K., Gordon, A. L., Hanratty, B., Towers, A. M., Irvine, L., Kelly,
S., Jones, L., Meyer, J., & Goodman, C. (2022). The uptake and use of a
minimum data set (MDS) for older people living and dying in care homes:
A realist review. *BMC Geriatrics*, *22*, Article 33. https://doi.org/10.1186/
s12877-021-02705-w

Na, E. (2022, June 14). Hongkongers are living longer than ever, but
experts flag health problems ahead. *South China Morning Post*. https://

www.scmp.com/news/hong-kong/society/article/3181505/hongkongers-are-living-longer-ever-experts-flag-health

Nabyonga-Orem, J. (2017). Monitoring Sustainable Development Goal 3: How ready are the health information systems in low-income and middle-income countries? *BMJ Global Health, 2*(4), Article e000433. https://doi.org/10.1136/bmjgh-2017-000433

Ng, F. (2019, September 15–16). *New model of 'internet + healthcare': Case study of online health* [Conference presentation abstract]. 7th International Jerusalem Conference on Health Policy, Jerusalem, Israel. https://doi.org/10.1186/s13584-019-0336-2

Ng, F., Briggs, D., & Liu, Y. (2022). Smart health communities: From sick care to health care. In B. Y. F. Fong, & M. C. S. Wong (Eds.), *The Routledge handbook of public health and the community* (pp. 302–312). Routledge. https://doi.org/10.4324/9781003119111-27-31

Ni, M. Y., Canudas-Romo, V., Shi, J., Flores, F. P., Chow, M. S., Yao, X. I.,... & Leung, G. M. (2021). Understanding longevity in Hong Kong: A comparative study with long-living, high-income countries. *The Lancet Public Health, 6*(12), e919-e931. https://doi.org/10.1016/S2468-2667(21)00208-5

Our World in Data. (2022). *Coronavirus (COVID-19) vaccinations.* Oxford Martin School. Retrieved August 20, 2022, from https://ourworldindata.org/covid-vaccinations#

Shukla. (2022, January 14). What is Web 1.0 Web 2.0 Web 3.0 Web 4.0 Web 5.0?. *DigitalGyan*. https://digitalgyan.org/what-is-web-1-0-web-2-0-web-3-0-web-4-0-web-5-0/

Sinovac. (n.d.). *Sinovac at glance*. http://www.sinovac.com/about/show.php?id=148&lang=en

The Global Health Observatory. (2022). *Life expectancy at birth (years)*. World Health Organization. Retrieved August 20, 2022, from https://www.who.int/data/gho/data/indicators/indicator-details/GHO/life-expectancy-at-birth-(years)

The Government of the Hong Kong Special Administrative Region. (2021, August 20). *eHRSS and eHealth App registered users exceed 4 million and 1.2 million respectively* [Press release]. https://www.info.gov.hk/gia/general/202108/20/P2021082000529.htm

Tin, P. (2022, March 30). COVID-19 highlights SAR's need for a comprehensive digital health blueprint. *Our Hong Kong Foundation*. https://www.ourhkfoundation.org.hk/en/report/36/healthcare-and-ageing/covid-19-highlights-sar%E2%80%99s-need-comprehensive-digital-health

United Nations. (2022). *Targets and indicators*. https://sdgs.un.org/goals/goal3

World Health Organization. (n.d.a). COVAX: *Working for global equitable access to COVID-19 vaccines*. https://www.who.int/initiatives/act-accelerator/covax

World Health Organization. (n.d.b). *Monitoring health for the SDGs*. https://www.who.int/data/gho/data/themes/world-health-statistics

World Health Organization. (n.d.c). *Substandard and falsified medical products*. https://www.who.int/health-topics/substandard-and-falsified-medical-products#tab=tab_2

World Health Organization. (2019). *Stronger collaboration, better health: Global action plan for healthy lives and well-being for all*. https://apps.who.int/iris/handle/10665/327841

World Health Organization. (2021). *Global strategy on digital health 2020-2025*. https://apps.who.int/iris/handle/10665/344249

Yoo, K. J., Mehta, A., Mak, J., Bishai, D., Chansa, C., & Patenaude, B. (2022). COVAX and equitable access to COVID-19 vaccines. *Bulletin of the World Health Organization, 100*(5), 315–328. https://doi.org/10.2471/BLT.21.287516

6 Leadership, Governance and SDG 3

Hilary H. L. Yee and Ben Y. F. Fong

Introduction

Unlike Millennium Development Goals that mainly targeted at developing countries, the implementation of the 2030 Agenda for Sustainable Development apply to all rich and poor countries. It provides a shared blueprint at a global level that involves partnerships between more than 70 governments. The 17 Sustainable Development Goals (SDGs) integrate with each other, and their complexities require holistic and coherent policymaking where decision-making and monitoring involve stakeholders from public and private sectors (Glass & Newig, 2019).

Among all SDGs, SDG 3 has been identified as a central role and received a much broader agenda for sustainable global development. Unprecedented growth of financial resources has been allocated in health sectors, and economic forces strongly influence public health policies (Missoni et al., 2019). Health systems and policies in different countries are complex, encompassing the provision of public and private health services, primary care, acute, chronic, long-term and aged care, in a variety of contexts. The 13 targets in SDG 3 are mostly qualitative and rely on how the governments decide their own policy to implement the goals.

To achieve SDG 3, governments need to create an environment for collective action and ensure parties and stakeholders involved are held accountable for the complex trade-offs between goals (Bowen et al., 2017). Lack of clarity, direction or competing frameworks can lead to policy confusion, resulting in ineffective health systems and service delivery (Brinkerhoff & Bossert, 2014). The outbreak of COVID-19 pandemic has highlighted that the lack of appropriate global health governance has contributed to surge in global infection rates, delay in the delivery and receiving timely and accurate information and failure

DOI: 10.4324/9781003305637-6

in distributing vaccines evenly among the rich and poor nations, as well as the International Health Regulations (IHR) not being complied with (Gostin et al., 2020). The pandemic has also revealed the wide disparity and inequality access of healthcare by race, ethnicity and socioeconomic status under poor governance in healthcare systems within countries (Perry et al., 2021).

Leadership and governance are therefore crucial elements for achieving SDG 3 at both the local and national levels. There are no universal definitions for leadership and governance in health. It is stated that the role of health leadership is to identify priorities, provide strategic direction and create commitment across the health sectors to achieve a common vision of healthcare services (Chunharas & Davies, 2016; Reich et al., 2016). Whereas governance is a multi-dimensional concept that covers different "processes, structures and institutions involved in political decision-making and implementation" (Fidler, 2010). The World Bank gives a precise definition on governance as a "the traditions and institutions by which authority in a country is exercised" (Kaufmann et al., 2011). Health governance is increasingly recognised as crucial factor in health system performance (Glass & Newig, 2019). It involves the distribution of roles and responsibilities and the implementation of collective actions to deal with health challenges and improvement (Brinkerhoff & Bossert, 2014).

In response to epidemiological, demographic and societal shifts, collaborative leadership and governance in which non-health and health sectors work together have become an international strategy to meet population needs (Chunharas & Davies, 2016; Figueroa et al., 2019). At this point, the World Health Organization (WHO) has long played an important role in gathering nations and countries together to work towards common health agenda and goals (Clift, 2013). Global health governance and SDG 3 implementation do not only require WHO's leadership in establishing, monitoring and enforcing international health standards, but also the close and committed cooperation among countries and regions.

The Role of WHO in SDG 3

In the health sector, governance in all countries is expected to be carried out under the direction of health ministries, while WHO has been responsible for providing leadership in global health matters for more than 70 years. It acts in an essential role in formulating norms and standards, articulating health policy options, providing technical supports to countries and assessing global health trends (United Nations,

2022). The concept of stewardship introduced by WHO more than 20 years ago has clarified the role of governance on effective healthcare systems around the world. WHO also plays a coordinating role in the IHR which is a legally-binding instrument of international law for 196 countries (World Health Organization, 2022a). The provision of strategic guidance and legal framework defines individual states' obligations in handling public health events and health security threats effectively, and achieving health-related goals (Brinkerhoff et al., 2019; Duff et al., 2021; World Health Organization, 2002).

To support SDG 3 in achieving the common health goals, WHO takes the lead in bringing multiple partners together, including donors, multilateral development organisations, non-government organisations (NGOs) and professional, research and academic organisations, together to meet the common health goals. For example, coordinated by WHO, 11 multilateral health, development and humanitarian agencies, including Woman, Children and Adolescents, The Global Fund to Fight AIDS, Tuberculosis and Malaria (The Global Fund), United Nations Children's Fund and World Bank Group, were teamed up to develop *Global Action Plan for Healthy Lives and Well-being for All* in order to accelerate progress towards health-related SDGs (World Health Organization, 2019a). WHO is also committed to ensuring statistical transparency and quality data are provided for countries and regions to achieve SDG 3. It releases the annual World Health Statistics Report which reports 50 health-related SDGs health statistics. Based on the latest health-related SDG indicators, WHO Member States can then monitor their progress towards SDG 3 more accurately and develop relevant policies more effectively.

In addition, WHO develops and endorses strategic framework for specific targets in SDG 3, for examples, *Ending Preventable Maternal Mortality Strategy* for target 3.1, a new version of *Global health sector strategy on HIV for 2016–2021* for target 3.3, and *Global Strategy on Human Resources for Health: Workforce 2030* for target 3c (World Health Organization, 2022b). To achieve target 3.3 of ending communicable diseases, WHO develops global guidance documents to help countries to scale up cost-effective interventions, diagnosis, treatment and prevention of infections (World Health Organization, 2015). Under the leadership of WHO, global infectious disease programmes have recorded a steep decline in the incidence of HIV, TB and malaria, the same situation even happened in the poor African countries (World Health Organization, 2015). This demonstrates that global health governance requires WHO's leadership and implementation of WHO's core global functions and frameworks to ensure effectiveness and success of all health actors.

Leadership and Governance Structure in Achieving Universal Health Coverage

SDG 3 targets to enhance health and well-being for all and a high-quality health system is an important component to achieving SDG 3 in all countries (Seidman, 2017). Health systems should optimise healthcare performance and be consistent in care delivery that meets healthcare needs of the population. The starting point for having a high-quality health system is moving towards universal health coverage (UHC), target 3.8 in SDG 3. Unlike countries with fragmented health systems, particularly with high out-of-pocket payment, strong leadership and governance in health systems often have resulted in successful UHC (Smith et al., 2012; Yip et al., 2019). Financed by mandatory contributions from taxation and social health insurance, countries like Australia, United Kingdom, Germany, Sweden and Switzerland have adopted different but effective governance in health system to expand equitable access to quality health services (Smith et al., 2012). Through adequate governance strategies like priority setting, monitoring, accountability and enforcement, the target of UHC in SDG 3 in these countries are achieved (Smith et al., 2012).

The question about which governance structure should be adopted to improve healthcare accessibility is always debatable in the literature (Carlson et al., 2015; Duff et al., 2021; Sheard et al., 2019). There is no definite answer to how governance in health should be structured, but successful leadership and governance of the health system would require features like priority setting, performance monitoring and accountability (Smith et al., 2012). Leadership and governance do not mean that a government itself needs to finance, provide or directly control resources in the health system (Smith et al., 2012). Rather, a government has the responsibility to ensure health-related goals are articulated, capacity of healthcare systems is in place, as well as stakeholders concerned are well prepared and committed to achieve the goals (Smith et al., 2012). Centralised decision-making allows better control of resources while delegation to decentralised units can identify and meet local health needs. The two countries below are examples demonstrating how different governance structures can be a conducive approach to achieving UHC in SDG 3.

Decentralised Healthcare Structure in Germany

Under the leadership of Otto von Bismark, health system reforms aimed at UHC in Germany started in the 1880s. He established the foundation of prepayment by workers and employers as social insurance, and introduced national health insurance as part of social security (Tulchinsky, 2018). The statutory health insurance system in Germany has compelled around 90% of the German population to participate in statutory health insurance, where coverage is universal and co-payments are moderate. Since 2004, the establishment of Federal Joint Committee has strengthened the principle of self-governance, where people can choose private insurance if their income exceeds the compulsory insurance threshold (Busse et al., 2017; Hullegie & Klein, 2010).

The Federal Joint Committee is a major payer-provider structure given the task of setting priorities, distributing of healthcare, and coordinating healthcare across sectors (Busse et al., 2017). Other key authorities in German healthcare include the National Association of Statutory Health Insurance Funds which represent the interests of health insurance funds at the federal level, the Institute for Quality and Efficiency in Health Care which is an independent organisation to assess benefits and risks on selected health topics using scientific data, the German Medical Association which is a joint association of 17 State Chambers of physicians, and the Institute for Applied Quality Improvement and Research in Health Care Gmbh that is responsible for quality assurance (Braithwaite et al., 2017).

The fundamental characteristic of public health system in Germany is structured as a federal, states and various corporatist institutions, delegating authorities at the local level with a strong degree of power in health decision making (Busse et al., 2017). The assigned authority of autonomous decision making allows local authorities to oversee broad health responsibilities, including infection prevention and control, hygiene monitoring and health promotion (Busse et al., 2017; Smith et al., 2012). In addition, authorities are required to make decisions that can balance the interests of different stakeholders, putting decision making and accountability together (Smith et al., 2012). Under this governance structure, payer and provider associations are well built, ensuring populations an equal access to high-quality healthcare without substantial shortages of health workers or waiting times in health treatment. The sharing of decision-making powers between the federal government, states, and local civil society organisations has brought Germany some early success in UHC.

Centralised Governance Structure in China

With the lack of strategic interactions among health providers and users, and provincial and local governments, the health reform during the 1980s in China was a failure (Ramesh et al., 2014). The fragmented healthcare governance is one of the major weaknesses in the health system at that time, when the responsibilities for healthcare were split across different agencies. To improve the situation, a major healthcare reform was launched in 2009, with the aim to provide healthcare with reasonable quality and expand social health insurance coverage for all (Yip et al., 2019). However, the decentralisation approach adopted during the early days of reform did not effectively structure a mechanism for controlling local governments in the delivery of adequate healthcare services to the local populations. Miscommunication among the multiple governing ministries resulted in conflicting policies, and physicians and hospitals were unfortunately only motivated by profit. There were no incentives to invest in population health (Ramesh et al., 2014). The Communist Party of China (CPC) then realised the need to restructure the mechanism for vertical co-ordination of healthcare and strengthen the position of health insurers (Ramesh et al., 2014).

The establishment of the National Healthcare Security Administration (NHSA) in 2018 had further restructured China's national health governance. NHSA then assumed the full responsibility of unifying the Urban Employee Basic Medical Insurance programme, Urban-Rural Resident Basic Medical Insurance programme and Medical Assistance. These authorities had functioned independently in the past (Tao et al., 2020; Yip et al., 2019). The insurance programmes were targeted for different population groups, namely workers and retirees, children, elderly, and the disabled. NHSA then manages the insurance schemes and health financing, while the National Health Commission handles the provision of healthcare, including planning, administration, and regulation in the health system (Yip et al., 2019). This re-centralised model has unified drug pricing, procurement, and distribution, as well as strengthened the governance in provincial and city-level governments in healthcare delivery. Most major health policies and strategies are proposed at CPC Congress, and hence, the success of the Chinese health system, to a certain extent, owes to the strong leadership of CPC (Wang et al., 2019).

The clear political willingness and commitment to people's livelihoods by the central government to achieve UHC by 2030 in China has made noteworthy progress in UHC, resulting in more than 95% of the population covered by basic health insurance schemes by 2018 (Tao et al., 2020). The increasing financial and human resources on health have allowed the population to utilise more adequate healthcare services and satisfy the unmet health needs. As a consequence, public health has contributed 77.9% to the increase of life expectancy among the populations in China (Tao et al., 2020; Wang et al., 2019).

China's top-level policy directives are visionary. However, this structure faces the danger of having weak or compromised local implementation, in which most provincial and city-level governments do not have the required resources to execute the specified health targets (Wang et al., 2019). Gaps remain in the lack of qualified healthcare workers, control of non-communicable diseases, efficiency in intersectoral actions, and development in the private health sector (Yip et al., 2019; Yuan et al., 2019). Despite the fact that healthcare reform has not reached its full potential, the governance and structural characteristics in China's health system have made remarkable contribution in its way to achieving UHC for one fifth of the world's population (Tao et al., 2020; Wang et al., 2019; Zhou et al., 2021).

Governance Commitment in SDG 3 – Reducing Maternal Mortality

The UN Target 3.1 of SDG 3 is to reduce global maternal mortality ratio to less than 70 per 100,000 live births. The high number of maternal mortality deaths in developing countries remain a major international concern (Okonofua et al., 2017; Victora et al., 2021). Low-income and lower-middle-income countries accounted for 99% of the global maternal deaths, and around 87% of global maternal deaths occurred in Sub-Saharan Africa and South Africa (Girum & Wasie, 2017). The high incidence reflects inadequate, unaffordable and unequal access to medical care among the women (World Health Organization, 2019b). The maternal mortality ratio fell by only 44% between 1990 and 2015, reflecting greater efforts are needed to reduce global maternal mortality. Successful interventions with strong effectiveness of governance and regulatory quality by governments in low-income countries had been shown to attain maternal mortality ratio similar to that of medium-income countries with lower governance (Ruiz-Cantero et al., 2019). This shows that greater governance would result in lower maternal mortality, independent of the country's income.

It has once been suggested that income of a country is a significant predictor of health status, including infant and maternal mortality (Ruiz-Cantero et al., 2019). However, studies based on The World Bank's six indicators on governance dimensions had found that maternal mortality was indeed associated with the quality of the government, including effectiveness of governance, corruption rate, voice accountability, level of democracy, absence of violence, and adherence to rule of law (Krueger et al., 2015; Pinzón-Flórez et al., 2015; Pinzon-Rondon et al., 2015). Income of a country is not an absolute determinant of maternal mortality and the quality of governance has confounding relationship with maternal mortality rates. If governments have the political will to prioritise the formulation and implementation of sexual and reproductive policies and to improve the quality of public services, reduction of maternal deaths could be achieved (Ruiz-Cantero et al., 2019).

Policy Prioritisation in Zimbabwe and Mexico

Zimbabwe is one of the Sub-Saharan Africa countries with high maternal mortality rate. HIV, obstetric haemorrhage, hypertensive disorders of pregnancy and obstetric trauma are common causes (Musarandega et al., 2022). Interventions were executed in Zimbabwe to tackle the problem by providing antiretroviral therapy, and training of nurses, midwives and doctors in comprehensive emergency obstetric and newborn care (Musarandega et al., 2022). To solve this critical threat to the achievement of SDG 3.1, WHO launched the Good Governance for Medicines and helped Zimbabwe to successfully conduct phase I of assessment through technical and financial support in late 2015 (Onwujekwe et al., 2019). However, like other countries in West African, corruption in the pharmaceutical sector and sub-optimal procurement of medical supplies for private use are common in Zimbabwe (Onwujekwe et al., 2019). Many local authorities have been accused of corruption with bad governance tendencies in allocating resources and handling public funds (Dziva & Kabonga, 2021; Verheul, 2021). In addition, the five-year implementation roadmap in Good Governance for Medicines starting from 2016 has been disrupted due to political interference of new officials (Onwujekwe et al., 2019). Evidence indicates that corruption in the health sector is distinctly dangerous and such poor governance has a significant effect in the infant and maternal mortality (Mhazo, & Maponga, 2022). Inequalities in utilisation of maternal health services due to wealth-related reasons among women in Zimbabwe remain, and the maternal mortality rate declines only in a gradual way over the years. Political prioritisation by national leaders in Zimbabwe may need to be reconsidered and re-visited in order to achieve greater implementation of SDGs (Dziva & Kabonga, 2021).

In Mexico, the government has set the minimisation of maternal mortality as one of its priorities within the healthcare system and health policy since the Millennium Development Goals initiatives

(Serván-Mori et al., 2021). Mexico government had mandated the reports of maternal deaths, conducted case analysis at the district level, and carried out epidemiological, cross-sectional and prospective studies to find out the causes of maternal deaths (Rodríguez-Aguilar, 2018; Williams, 2020). Inequity of access to health services and poverty were identified as major factors causing maternal mortality. Therefore, health reforms and pertinent policies to improve healthcare access had been implemented in the Mexican health system. The government established a public insurance called *Seguro Popular* in 2003. This Social Health Protection System reform was designed to expand health protection to uninsured women, including those who are self-employed, underemployed, and unemployed (Servan-Mori et al., 2016; Serván-Mori et al., 2021). Other programmes called PROSPERA and *Programa Arranque Perojo en Ia Vida* had empowered women to manage their health by providing them self-healthcare during pregnancy and childbirth, health education and health clinic registration (Rodríguez-Aguilar, 2018). Together with interventions on early detection of diseases for children, family planning and contraception, noteworthy progress has been achieved in the coverage of the continuum of maternal healthcare in Mexico, and maternal mortality rate has decreased 56% from 1990 to 2014 (Rodríguez-Aguilar, 2018).

The Continuing Pathway to Achieving SDG 3

In recent years, it is getting more difficult to gather cooperation among countries. WHO's leading role in improving global health has been plagued by competing economic, political, and social demands (Benvenisti, 2020). Nevertheless, new international initiatives such as the World Bank, the JointUnited Nations Programmes on HIV/AIDS, the Global Alliance for Vaccines, Roll Back Malaria and The Global Fund have entered the global health sector to promote the development of global health partnerships (Clift, 2013; Van de Pas et al., 2017). An increasing number of public-private partnerships, and non-governmental partners are developed to tackle specific global health issues, challenging the role of WHO as the directing and coordinating authority (Clift, 2013). Although WHO is the only administrator of the legally binding international health regulations, its authority and capacity to lead international responses, like during the outbreak of Ebola and COVID-19 pandemic, have been questioned (Kuznetsova, 2020). WHO has also encountered political confrontation such as the United States' suspension of financing and withdrawal of her membership from the organisation. This has led other Member States such as China, Germany and France to provide extra funding to support the WHO (Kuznetsova, 2020). This incident has revealed that WHO strongly relies on global partnerships and commitment for its leadership role and resources. Though WHO was first designed on an assumption that the responsibility to improve global health would be shared by all nations, this ideal concept has been affected by competing economic and political cooperation among the countries.

The 2030 Agenda for SDGs encourages countries to "conduct regular and inclusive review of progress at the national and local levels, which are country-led and country-driven", in order to build more effective and well-performed health governance systems towards achieving SDG 3 (Morita et al., 2020). To accelerate the efforts in reaching all SDGs, including SDG 3, effective rule of law and good governance at all levels, as well as horizontal and vertical policy coherence, are required. Apart from WHO, international organisations and networks such as United Nations Development Group and Organization for Economic Co-operation and Development have also provided guidelines for policy-makers to support national implementation of SDGs (Morita et al., 2020). Although these guidelines provide some key elements like health screening tools and ways to strengthen partnerships for different health sectors, they do not illustrate a tailored approach that is directly applicable to the circumstances in various countries (Morita et al., 2020). Afterall, every country should identify the weaknesses and strengths in their governance systems and leadership, and then determine their own priorities for health needs and interventions to achieve SDG 3.

Lower income countries generally lack leadership, managerial capacity and the required governance competencies to improve health services. Notwithstanding that each country should be responsible for their own achievement towards SDG 3. Higher income countries are encouraged to exercise the spirit of mutual funding and assistance to low-income countries for them to carry out sustainable health interventions and programmes. For instance, the six-year (2017–2022) Transform: Primary Health Care Activity funded by the United States Agency for International Development has supported the government of Ethiopia to improve the health management system (Argaw et al., 2021). The leadership, management, and governance intervention implemented has enhanced knowledge and skills for more health workers in primary care, and effectively reduced maternal and child health service performance (Argaw et al., 2021). To achieve SDG 3, all countries are called upon to develop a more integrated and holistic health governance. In addition, SDG 3 can only be realised with a stronger global cooperation and commitment by all nations. All countries should build their individual health systems upon a shared vision and goals, placing people's health at the centre.

References

Argaw, M. D., Desta, B. F., Muktar, S. A., Abera, W. S., Beshir, I. A., Otoro, I. A.,... & Eifler, K. (2021). Comparison of maternal and child health service performances following a leadership, management, and governance intervention in Ethiopia: A propensity score matched analysis. *BMC Health Services Research, 21,* Article 862. https://doi.org/10.1186/s12913-021-06873-8

Benvenisti, E. (2020). The WHO—Destined to fail?: Political cooperation and the COVID-19 pandemic. *American Journal of International Law, 114*(4), 588–597. https://doi.org/10.1017/ajil.2020.66

Braithwaite, J., Matsuyama, Y., & Johnson, J. (2017). *Healthcare reform, quality and safety: Perspectives, participants, partnerships and prospects in 30 countries.* CRC Press. https://doi.org/10.1201/9781315586373

Brinkerhoff, D. W., & Bossert, T. J. (2014). Health governance: principal–agent linkages and health system strengthening. *Health Policy and Planning, 29*(6), 685–693. https://doi.org/10.1093/heapol/czs132

Brinkerhoff, D. W., Cross, H. E., Sharma, S., & Williamson, T. (2019). Stewardship and health systems strengthening: An overview. *Public Administration and Development, 39*(1), 4–10. https://doi.org/10.1002/pad.1846

Busse, R., Blümel, M., Knieps, F., & Bärnighausen, T. (2017). Statutory health insurance in Germany: A health system shaped by 135 years of solidarity, self-governance, and competition. *The Lancet, 390*(10097), 882–897. https://doi.org/10.1016/S0140-6736(17)31280-1

Carlson, V., Chilton, M. J., Corso, L. C., & Beitsch, L. M. (2015). Defining the functions of public health governance. *American Journal of Public Health, 105*(S2), S159–S166. https://doi.org/10.2105/AJPH.2014.302198

Chunharas, S., & Davies, D. S. C. (2016). Leadership in health systems: A new agenda for interactive leadership. *Health Systems & Reform, 2*(3), 176–178. https://doi.org/10.1080/23288604.2016.1222794

Clift, C. (2013). *The role of the World Health Organization in the international system.* https://www.chathamhouse.org/sites/default/files/publications/research/2013-02-01-role-world-health-organization-international-system-clift.pdf

Duff, J. H., Liu, A., Saavedra, J., Batycki, J. N., Morancy, K., Stocking, B.,... & Szapocznik, J. (2021). A global public health convention for the 21st century. *The Lancet Public Health, 6*(6), e428–e433. https://doi.org/10.1016/S2468-2667(21)00070-0

Dziva, C., & Kabonga, I. (2021). Opportunities and challenges for local government institutions in localising sustainable development goals in Zimbabwe. In G. Nhamo, M. Togo, & K. Dube (Eds.), *Sustainable*

Development Goals for Society (Vol. 1, pp. 219–233). Springer, Cham. https://doi.org/10.1007/978-3-030-70948-8_15

Figueroa, C. A., Harrison, R., Chauhan, A., & Meyer, L. (2019). Priorities and challenges for health leadership and workforce management globally: A rapid review. *BMC Health Services Research, 19*, Article 239. https://doi.org/10.1186/s12913-019-4080-7

Girum, T., & Wasie, A. (2017). Correlates of maternal mortality in developing countries: An ecological study in 82 countries. *Maternal Health, Neonatology and Perinatology, 3*, Article 19. https://doi.org/10.1186/s40748-017-0059-8

Glass, L. M., & Newig, J. (2019). Governance for achieving the sustainable development goals: How important are participation, policy coherence, reflexivity, adaptation and democratic institutions? *Earth System Governance, 2*, Article 100031. https://doi.org/10.1016/j.esg.2019.100031

Gostin, L. O., Moon, S., & Meier, B. M. (2020). Reimagining global health governance in the age of COVID-19. *American Journal of Public Health, 110*(11), 1615–1619. https://doi.org/10.2105/AJPH.2020.305933

Hullegie, P., & Klein, T. J. (2010). The effect of private health insurance on medical care utilization and self-assessed health in Germany. *Health Economics, 19*(9), 1048–1062. https://doi.org/10.1002/hec.1642

Kaufmann, D., Kraay, A., & Mastruzzi, M. (2011). The worldwide governance indicators: Methodology and analytical issues1. *Hague Journal on the Rule of Law, 3*(2), 220–246. https://doi.org/10.1017/S1876404511200046

Krueger, P. M., Dovel, K., & Denney, J. T. (2015). Democracy and self-rated health across 67 countries: A multilevel analysis. *Social Science & Medicine, 143*, 137–144. https://doi.org/10.1016/j.socscimed.2015.08.047

Kuznetsova, L. (2020). COVID-19: The world community expects the World Health Organization to play a stronger leadership and coordination role in pandemics control. *Frontiers in Public Health, 8*, Article 470. https://doi.org/10.3389/fpubh.2020.00470

Mhazo, A. T., & Maponga, C. C. (2022). The importance of prioritizing politics in Good Governance for Medicines Initiative in Zimbabwe: A qualitative policy analysis study. *Health Policy and Planning, 37*(5), 634–643. https://doi.org/10.1093/heapol/czac007

Missoni, E., Pacileo, G., & Tediosi, F. (2019). *Global health governance and policy: An introduction*. Routledge. https://doi.org/10.4324/9781351188999

Morita, K., Okitasari, M., & Masuda, H. (2020). Analysis of national and local governance systems to achieve the sustainable development goals: Case studies of Japan and Indonesia. *Sustainability Science, 15*(1), 179–202. https://doi.org/10.1007/s11625-019-00739-z

Musarandega, R., Ngwenya, S., Murewanhema, G., Machekano, R., Magwali, T., Nystrom, L.,... & Munjanja, S. (2022). Changes in causes of pregnancy-related and maternal mortality in Zimbabwe 2007–08 to 2018–19: Findings from two reproductive age mortality surveys. *BMC Public Health, 22*, Article 923. https://doi.org/10.1186/s12889-022-13321-7

Okonofua, F. E., Ntoimo, L. F. C., & Ogu, R. N. (2018). Women's perceptions of reasons for maternal deaths: Implications for policies and programs for preventing maternal deaths in low-income countries. *Health Care for Women International, 39*(1), 95–109. https://doi.org/10.1080/07399332.2017. 1365868

Onwujekwe, O., Agwu, P., Orjiakor, C., McKee, M., Hutchinson, E., Mbachu, C.,... & Balabanova, D. (2019). Corruption in Anglophone West Africa health systems: A systematic review of its different variants and the factors that sustain them. *Health Policy and Planning, 34*(7), 529–543. https://doi. org/10.1093/heapol/czz070

Perry, B. L., Aronson, B., & Pescosolido, B. A. (2021). Pandemic precarity: COVID-19 is exposing and exacerbating inequalities in the American heartland. *Proceedings of the National Academy of Sciences, 118*(8). https:// doi.org/10.1073/pnas.2020685118

Pinzón-Flórez, C. E., Fernández-Niño, J. A., Ruiz-Rodríguez, M., Idrovo, Á. J., & Arredondo López, A. A. (2015). Determinants of performance of health systems concerning maternal and child health: A global approach. *PLoS One, 10*(3), Article e0120747. https://doi.org/10.1371/journal.pone.0120747

Pinzon-Rondon, A. M., Attaran, A., Botero, J. C., & Ruiz-Sternberg, A. M. (2015). Association of rule of law and health outcomes: An ecological study. *BMJ Open, 5*(10), Article e007004. https://doi.org/10.1136/ bmjopen-2014-007004

Ramesh, M., Wu, X., & He, A. J. (2014). Health governance and healthcare reforms in China. *Health Policy and Planning, 29*(6), 663–672. https://doi. org/10.1093/heapol/czs109

Reich, M. R., Javadi, D., & Ghaffar, A. (2016). Introduction to the special issue on "effective leadership for health systems". *Health Systems & Reform, 2*(3), 171–175. https://doi.org/10.1080/23288604.2016.1223978

Rodríguez-Aguilar, R. (2018). Maternal mortality in Mexico, beyond millennial development objectives: An age-period-cohort model. *PLoS One, 13*(3), Article e0194607. https://doi.org/10.1371/journal.pone.0194607

Ruiz-Cantero, M. T., Guijarro-Garvi, M., Bean, D. R., Martínez-Riera, J. R., & Fernández-Sáez, J. (2019). Governance commitment to reduce maternal mortality. A political determinant beyond the wealth of the countries. *Health & Place, 57,* 313–320. https://doi.org/10.1016/j.healthplace.2019.05.012

Seidman, G. (2017). Does SDG 3 have an adequate theory of change for improving health systems performance? *Journal of Global Health, 7*(1), Article 010302. https://doi.org/10.7189/jogh.07.010302

Servan-Mori, E., Avila-Burgos, L., Nigenda, G., & Lozano, R. (2016). A performance analysis of public expenditure on maternal health in Mexico. *PLoS One, 11*(4), Article e0152635. https://doi.org/10.1371/journal.pone.0152635

Serván-Mori, E., Heredia-Pi, I., García, D. C., Nigenda, G., Sosa-Rubí, S. G., Seiglie, J. A., & Lozano, R. (2021). Assessing the continuum of care for maternal health in Mexico, 1994–2018. *Bulletin of the World Health Organization, 99*(3), 190–200. https://doi.org/10.2471/BLT.20.252544

96   *Hilary H. L. Yee and Ben Y. F. Fong*

Sheard, D. J., Clydesdale, G., & Maclean, G. (2019). Governance structure and public health provision. *Journal of Health Organization and Management, 33*(4), 426–442. https://doi.org/10.1108/JHOM-11-2018-0336

Smith, P. C., Anell, A., Busse, R., Crivelli, L., Healy, J., Lindahl, A. K.,... & Kene, T. (2012). Leadership and governance in seven developed health systems. *Health Policy, 106*(1), 37–49. https://doi.org/10.1016/j.healthpol.2011.12.009

Tao, W., Zeng, Z., Dang, H., Lu, B., Chuong, L., Yue, D.,... & Kominski, G. F. (2020). Towards universal health coverage: Lessons from 10 years of health-care reform in China. *BMJ Global Health, 5*(3), Article e002086. http://doi.org/10.1136/bmjgh-2019-002086

Tulchinsky, T. H. (2018). Bismarck and the long road to universal health coverage. In T. H. Tulchinsky (Ed.), *Case Studies in Public Health* (pp. 131–179). Academic Press. https://doi.org/10.1016/B978-0-12-804571-8.00031-7

United Nations. (2022). *WHO: World Health Organisation.* https://www.un.org/youthenvoy/2013/09/who-world-health-organisation/

Van de Pas, R., Hill, P. S., Hammonds, R., Ooms, G., Forman, L., Waris, A.,... & Sridhar, D. (2017). Global health governance in the sustainable development goals: Is it grounded in the right to health? *Global Challenges, 1*(1), 47–60. https://doi.org/10.1002/gch2.1022

Victora, C. G., Christian, P., Vidaletti, L. P., Gatica-Domínguez, G., Menon, P., & Black, R. E. (2021). Revisiting maternal and child undernutrition in low-income and middle-income countries: Variable progress towards an unfinished agenda. *The Lancet, 397*(10282), 1388–1399. https://doi.org/10.1016/S0140-6736(21)00394-9

Verheul, S. (2021). From 'defending sovereignty' to 'fighting corruption': The political place of law in Zimbabwe after November 2017. *Journal of Asian and African Studies, 56*(2), 189–203. https://doi.org/10.1177/0021909620986587

Wang, L., Wang, Z., Ma, Q., Fang, G., & Yang, J. (2019). The development and reform of public health in China from 1949 to 2019. *Globalization and Health, 15,* Article 45. https://doi.org/10.1186/s12992-019-0486-6

Williams, S. A. (2020). Narratives of responsibility: Maternal mortality, reproductive governance, and midwifery in Mexico. *Social Science & Medicine, 254,* Article 112227. https://doi.org/10.1016/j.socscimed.2019.03.023

World Health Organization. (2000). *The world health report 2000: health systems: Improving performance.* https://apps.who.int/iris/bitstream/handle/10665/42281/WHR_2000-eng.pdf?sequence=1&isAllowed=y

World Health Organization. (2015). *Accelerating progress on HIV, tuberculosis, malaria, hepatitis and neglected tropical diseases.* http://apps.who.int/iris/bitstream/handle/10665/204419/9789241510134_eng.pdf;jsessionid=2757C8EDE5AA1FBC857F720110C8F2DD?sequence=1

World Health Organization. (2019a). *Stronger collaboration, better health.* https://www.who.int/publications/i/item/9789241516433

World Health Organization. (2019b). *Maternal mortality: Evidence brief* (No. WHO/RHR/19.20). World Health Organization. https://apps.who.int/iris/bitstream/handle/10665/329886/WHO-RHR-19.20-eng.pdf

World Health Organization. (2022a). *International health regulations.* https://www.who.int/health-topics/international-health-regulations#tab=tab_1

World Health Organization. (2022b). *Monitoring health for the SDGs.* https://www.who.int/data/gho/data/themes/sustainable-development-goals?lang=en/

Yip, W., Fu, H., Chen, A. T., Zhai, T., Jian, W., Xu, R.,... & Chen, W. (2019). 10 years of health-care reform in China: Progress and gaps in universal health coverage. *The Lancet, 394*(10204), 1192–1204. https://doi.org/10.1016/S0140-6736(19)32136-1

Yuan, B., Balabanova, D., Gao, J., Tang, S., & Guo, Y. (2019). Strengthening public health services to achieve universal health coverage in China. *BMJ, 365*, Article 12358. https://doi.org/10.1136/bmj.12358

Zhou, S., Huang, T., Li, A., & Wang, Z. (2021). Does universal health insurance coverage reduce unmet healthcare needs in China? Evidence from the National Health Service Survey. *International Journal for Equity in Health, 20*, Article 43. https://doi.org/10.1186/s12939-021-01385-7

Index

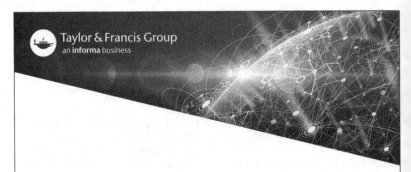

Printed in the United States
by Baker & Taylor Publisher Services